Logic Puzzles Book for Kids Age 10 to 13

Difficult Brain Teasers Puzzles for Smart Kids

PuzzleLoco Press

Special Offer

Join Our Launch Club and Get Future Puzzle Books 100% FREE!

Want our future puzzle books delivered straight to you?

Hundreds of others are already enjoying access to all of our current and future puzzle and logic books, 100% free!

If you want insider access PLUS free puzzle books for any occasion, all you have to do is scan the code below to claim your offer!

Introduction

PuzzleLoco Press was born from our increased desire for on-demand reality television and discovering our handwriting was starting to suck.

Good habits start small. This puzzle book will:

- train your attention span
- improve your vocabulary
- and teach you what a pencil was used for back in the day.

You bought this book. You're on the right track.

This logic book was designed for really, really smart kids!

One of our biggest complaints about our children's books is that "That was too easy!"

So we compiled a combination of brain-bustin' logic puzzles meant to stump and frustrate you, until you put it down and pick it back up again.

Good luck!

Table of Contents

Grid Puzzles

With only the clues given, can you use logical deduction to find each item's match?

There are 3 categories of items you must match up.

Each category can use each item only once, and there are no duplicates.

		Category #2					Category #3				
		Item #1	Item #2	Item #3	Item #4	Item #5	Item #1	Item #2	Item #3	Item #4	Item #5
Category #1	Item #1										
	Item #2										
	Item #3										
	Item #4										
	Item #5										
Category #3	Item #1										
	Item #2										
	Item #3										
	Item #4										
	Item #5										

Clue Example:
1. **[CATEGORY 1 ITEM #3]**'s **book**, due **[CATEGORY 3 ITEM #3]**, is not **[CATEGORY 2 ITEM #1]** or **[CATEGORY 2 ITEM #2]**.

Category #1	Category #2	Category #3

Hints for Solving:

Each item has exactly one possible match within its category, and no two items from the same category will ever have a common match in another category.

The objective is to determine which items belong with which by using only the provided hints and your own deductive reasoning skills.

Each puzzle has 3 categories. Look at how the Category #3 is repeated on the left and top. This design is used for all grids in logic puzzles.

Why do we do this? The purpose of a logic grid is to establish whether or not two items are matched. With the categories set up in this way, there is only one possible set of combinations between any two given grid cells.

#1

		Book Title					Due Date				
		Loaded Veil	The Voice	Death Of Bo	Made 4 You	Money Hand	November 21	November 30	December 5	December 12	December 19
Students	Daryl										
	Hannah										
	Amanda										
	Jacob										
	Bryan										
Due Date	November 21										
	November 30										
	December 5										
	December 12										
	December 19										

The Clues:

1. Amanda's book, due the first week of December, is not "The Voice" or "Loaded Veil."
2. Jacob's book is due 1 week before Amanda's.
3. Bryan's book, "Loaded Veil" is due in November.
4. Daryl did not check out "Death of Bo" or "Money Hand."
5. Hannah's book, "Death of Bo" is due 1 week after Amanda's.
6. Amanda's is book "Made For You."

Students	Book Title	Due Date

#2

		Placements					Town				
		1st	2nd	3rd	4th	5th	Denver	Houston	NYC	San Diego	Miami
Contestant	Josh										
	Brad										
	Diane										
	Rose										
	Taylor										
Town	Denver										
	Houston										
	NYC										
	San Diego										
	Miami										

The Clues:

1. Josh, who finished right before Brad, is from this New England city.
2. Taylor, who came in 1st place, finished the race right before the contestant from Houston.
3. Rose, who finished before Josh, is from Miami.
4. Taylor is not from San Diego.
5. Diane came in 2 places before the contestant from NYC, who came in 4th.
6. The contestant from San Diego came in last place, while Houston was in 2nd.

Contestant	Placements	Town

#3

		Month					Color				
		March	April	May	June	July	Blue	Red	Green	Purple	Yellow
Name	Benny										
	Dover										
	Gaia										
	Brad										
	Cliff										
Color	Blue										
	Red										
	Green										
	Purple										
	Yellow										

The Clues:
1. Benny hates the color green and was born in July.
2. Cliff was not born in March and loves Yellow.
3. Dover's favorite color is Red and was born in April.
4. Gaia loves Blue and was born a month before Dover.
5. Brad was born in May and does not like Red.

Name	Month	Color

#4

		Movie					Showtime				
		Spacebird	Haunted	Traitors	A Love Story	Zombiebus	12:45pm	1:15pm	2:15pm	2:45pm	3:30pm
Name	Jack										
	Jason										
	Josh										
	Jim										
	Joseph										
Showtime	12:45pm										
	1:15pm										
	2:15pm										
	2:45pm										
	3:30pm										

The Clues:

1. Josh's movie "Traitors" starts 2 hours after Joseph's, which starts at 12:45pm.
2. The latest showtime is for "Zombiebus."
3. Jim is watching "A Love Story" at 1:15pm.
4. Jason's movie, "Spacebird," starts 1 hour later than Jim's.
5. Jack's movie has the latest showtime because he couldn't leave practice early.

Name	Movie	Showtime

#5

		Location					Month				
		Hawaii	Florida	Colorado	Maine	Oregon	January	March	May	August	November
Employee	Don										
	Ron										
	Sandy										
	Carol										
	Daryl										
Month	January										
	March										
	May										
	August										
	November										

The Clues:

1. Don is taking a vacation to the West Coast the month after Christmas.
2. Sandy almost went to Florida for the summer but decided on the Rocky Mountains instead.
3. Carol's vacation to Florida is conveniently after the end of summer.
4. Ron is visiting his family in New England for Thanksgiving.
5. Daryl's island vacation is in March.

Employee	Location	Month

7

#6

		Fruit					Price				
		Apple	Banana	Orange	Grapes	Lemon	50 Cents	75 Cents	$1	$1.25	$1.50
Name	Lydia										
	Rich										
	Monica										
	Mimi										
	Cisco										
Price	50 Cents										
	75 Cents										
	$1										
	$1.25										
	$1.50										

The Clues:

1. Monica's apple cost $1 less than Lydia's banana, which costs $1.50.
2. Cisco, who is allergic to oranges, would never spend more than $1 on fruit.
3. Mimi plans to use her fruit to open a lemonade stand.
4. Rich's orange cost the same as the apple and grapes combined.
5. The grapes cost 75 cents, and the apple is the cheapest fruit.

Name	Fruit	Price

#7

	Placements					Color				
	1st	2nd	3rd	4th	5th	Blue	Red	Green	Purple	Yellow
Team Bulldogs										
Tridents										
Foghorns										
Rebels										
Hooziers										
Color Blue										
Red										
Green										
Purple										
Yellow										

The Clues:

1. The team that won used Red paintballs.
2. The Foghorns placed 3 spots ahead of the team that used Green paintballs.
3. 3rd place was not Purple or Blue.
4. The Tridents, who were last, weren't blue or red, but rather, a combination.
5. The Rebels placed two spots behind the Hooziers, who placed 2nd and used Blue paintballs.

Team	Placements	Color

9

#8

	Customer	Car					Length				
		Toyota	Honda	Ford	Dodge	Kia	2 Days	3 Days	4 Days	5 Days	6 Days
Customer	Brenda										
	Sean										
	Blake										
	Sonja										
	Jamie										
Length	2 Days										
	3 Days										
	4 Days										
	5 Days										
	6 Days										

The Clues:
1. Brenda is keeping the Dodge 2 days longer than Jamie's Kia, which is a 2-day rental.
2. Sonja specifically asked she not receive a Ford or a Honda.
3. Sean is keeping his car half the time that Sonja has hers.
4. The Ford was rented 3 days longer than the Kia.
5. Blake did not have the Toyota or Honda.

Customer	Car	Length

#9

		Order					Price				
		Mocha	Latte	Americano	Iced Coffee	Tea	$2.10	$2.20	$2.40	$2.50	$2.80
Customer	Dustin										
	Lee										
	Iris										
	Chuck										
	Ramona										
Price	$2.10										
	$2.20										
	$2.40										
	$2.50										
	$2.80										

The Clues:

1. Ramona's iced coffee cost 40 cents more than Lee's mocha.
2. Chuck, who ordered a tea, spent 60 cents more than the Americano.
3. Iris' latte cost 20 cents more than Dustin's drink.
4. Lee spent the least amount of money.

Customer	Order	Price

#10

		Pet					Cost				
		Dog	Cat	Iguana	Hamster	Parrot	$50	$75	$95	$110	$125
Name	Marge										
	Homer										
	Bart										
	Lisa										
	Maggie										
Cost	$50										
	$75										
	$95										
	$110										
	$125										

The Clues:

1. Marge, who chose a parrot, spent $50 less than Maggie.
2. Lisa's dog cost $15 more than Homer's cat.
3. Homer was happy to spend $20 more than Marge.
4. Bart could only afford the hamster.

Name	Pet	Cost

Solution: **#1**

Jacob   ->   Money Hand   ->   November 30

Bryan   ->   Loaded Veil   ->   November 21

Amanda   ->   Made 4 You   ->   December 5

Hannah   ->   Death Of Bo   ->   December 12

Daryl   ->   The Voice   ->   December 19

Solution: **#2**

Brad   ->   5th   ->   San Diego

Josh   ->   4th   ->   NYC

Diane   ->   2nd   ->   Houston

Rose   ->   3rd   ->   Miami

Taylor   ->   1st   ->   Denver

Solution: # #3

Benny -> July -> Purple

Gaia -> March -> Blue

Dover -> April -> Red

Brad -> May -> Green

Cliff -> June -> Yellow

Solution: # #4

Joseph -> Haunted -> 12:45pm

Jason -> Spacebird -> 2:15pm

Josh -> Traitors -> 2:45pm

Jim -> A Love Story -> 1:15pm

Jack -> Zombiebus -> 3:30pm

Solution: # #5

Daryl   ->   Hawaii   ->   March

Don ->   Oregon   ->   January

Sandy ->   Colorado   ->   May

Ron ->   Maine   ->   November

Carol ->   Florida   ->   August

Solution: # #6

Monica   ->   Apple   ->   50 Cents

Lydia   ->   Banana   -> $1.50

Cisco ->   Grapes   ->   75 Cents

Rich   ->   Orange   -> $1.25

Mimi   ->   Lemon   -> $1

Solution: # #7

Rebels -> 4th -> Green

Tridents -> 5th -> Purple

Foghorns -> 1st -> Red

Hooziers -> 2nd -> Blue

Bulldogs -> 3rd -> Yellow

Solution: # #8

Brenda -> Dodge -> 4 Days

Sean -> Honda -> 3 Days

Jamie -> Kia -> 2 Days

Blake -> Ford -> 5 Days

Sonja -> Toyota -> 6 Days

#9

Solution:

Ramona -> Iced Coffee -> $2.50

Dustin -> Americano -> $2.20

Lee -> Mocha -> $2.10

Iris -> Latte -> $2.40

Chuck -> Tea -> $2.80

#10

Solution:

Marge -> Parrot -> $75

Maggie -> Iguana -> $125

Lisa -> Dog -> $110

Bart -> Hamster -> $50

Homer -> Cat -> $95

Word Blocks

When playing Word Blocks, you'll be presented with a grid containing hints along each row and 2x2 letter blocks to fill it in.

ACCUSES

BANISHED PEOPLE

BEAT IT

BECOMES OF USE

ACCEPTED BELIEFS

0 THROUGH 9

CHICKEN SCRATCH

A CARNIVAL WORKER

APPLE FLAW

COCKTAIL SHAKER

N	I
A	I

S	C
B	A

A	M
I	L

A	S
T	S

W	L
E	R

B	L
E	X

G	M
G	I

S	H
L	S

D	O
D	I

S	E
A	N

V	A
A	V

U	I
R	M

E	S
E	S

B	R
B	A

R	A
R	K

#1

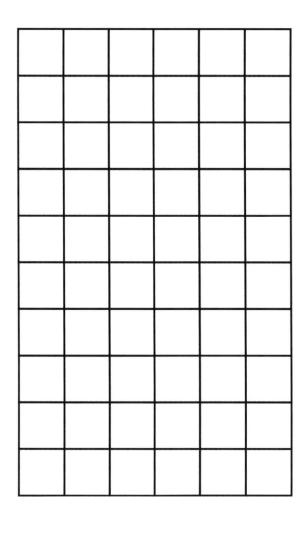

BUYOFFS

CERTAIN DRESS CODE

ANTENNA TYPE

DIDN'T HAVE

"IN CONCLUSION..."

ARRANGED IN TWOS

ACTED THE VALET

DELUGE

AMARETTO FLAVOR

"I DO" SETTING

L	Y
E	D

N	D
E	L

P	A
D	R

E	S
A	L

R	K
E	N

D	I
L	A

I	B
S	U

A	L
C	H

B	R
C	A

M	O
A	P

L	A
P	A

L	E
E	D

P	O
C	K

E	D
C	H

S	T
I	R

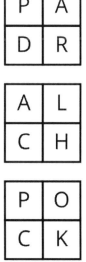

#2

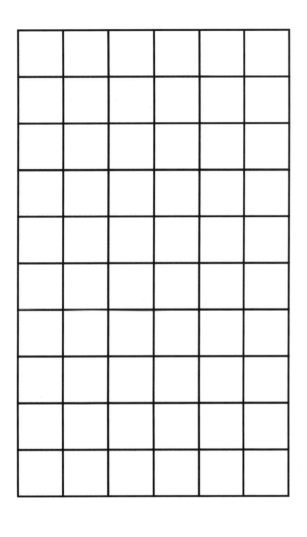

ENCOURAGEMENTS

OLYMPIC SPORT

ACCOUNTING STATS

LESS TACKY

APPARENTLY SUITABLE

HOT

KIND OF GOWN

ARCHER

WENT AGAINST

ACCEPTABLE TO EAT

A	L
A	N

E	S
E	R

K	E
K	I

L	I
B	A

E	D
L	E

B	U
E	D

T	S
N	G

L	O
A	R

B	O
D	I

L	Y
N	G

B	R
B	O

I	D
W	M

S	S
T	I

O	S
V	I

C	K
I	B

#3

ABANDON

BOZOS

BLOTS OUT

AUTHORED

ADVANCES LIKE IVY

AROSE, AS A STORM

MIDDLEMAN.

BAD POSTURES

ATTIC OPENING

ABUNDANCE

E	E
E	W

V	A
J	O

L	S
E	D

C	R
B	R

E	R
T	Y

P	S
E	D

C	A
K	E

A	N
P	E

B	B
O	O

R	M
U	N

D	O
B	O

E	R
P	S

N	U
N	N

T	E
R	S

J	O
S	T

#4

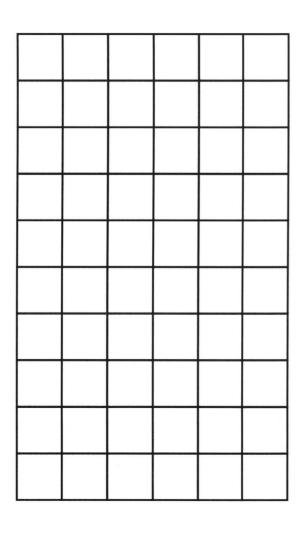

LESS CHICKEN

ADDS COLOR TO

AWNING

ADJUSTS

CHARACTERIZE

BERING --

AID TO NAVIGATORS

AD FORM

BANQUET DELICACY

BICYCLE FEATURES

A	R
L	S

B	R
S	T

C	A
A	L

E	R
N	S

P	Y
N	S

V	I
D	A

D	E
S	T

O	N
E	R

F	I
R	A

N	E
I	T

B	E
B	A

A	V
A	I

A	C
N	N

C	A
P	E

N	O
I	G

#5

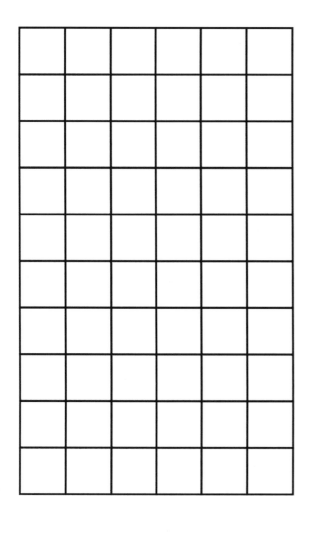

BACKUP

"IN CONCLUSION..."

COFFEE MEASURE

BEFORE NINTH

AROUSE

HOT

ASSOCIATES

ARRANGEMENT

AMOUNTS BEING BET

FREE LOADER.

A	K
D	G

T	E
N	G

S	T
C	A

L	O
L	A

E	S
E	R

G	J
S	T

C	I
K	I

A	L
L	A

U	L
T	H

P	F
G	H

C	U
E	I

E	X
B	A

L	I
Y	O

E	S
U	T

A	M
L	Y

#6

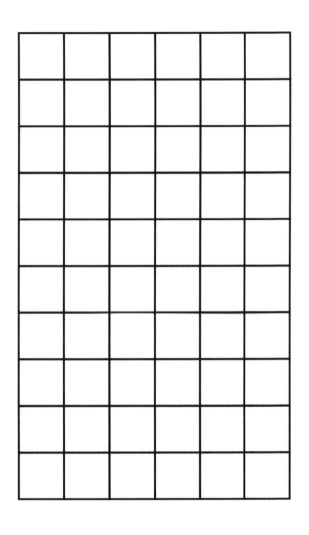

ENGAGINGLY INNOCENT

DELUGE

A COLOR BLUE

BE ACCOMMODATING

COFFEE MEASURE

BACKS FINANCIALLY

AIRHEADS

CAREFULLY EXAMINED

"AMEN!"

ACCEPTED DOCTRINE

P	F
D	O

L	T
S	T

C	U
E	N

D	U
S	C

S	H
C	H

C	O
A	D

B	A
J	U

R	E
L	I

E	D
E	F

N	C
O	P

B	O
D	R

A	G
B	E

E	S
E	D

U	L
W	S

Y	I
E	N

#7

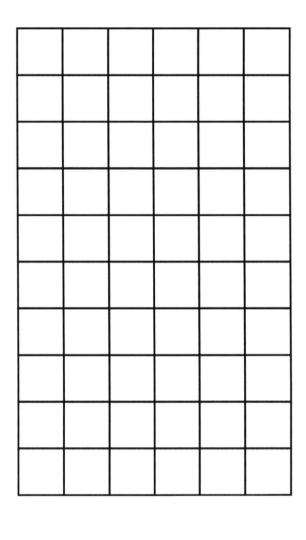

FAIR WAY TO SHARE

CREATED OR INVENTED

AGENCY

BOX AT THE GYM?

BOOZEHOUNDS

BOARDER

ACCOUNTING JOBS

ADHESIVE SURFACE.

BIG FINISH

CHECKED FOR PRINTS

R	E
C	K

K	S
E	R

I	M
S	T

L	Y
E	D

B	U
L	O

A	U
E	R

T	S
N	T

C	L
D	U

E	V
C	O

A	U
C	E

D	R
L	O

D	I
M	E

U	N
D	G

A	X
E	D

E	N
I	N

#8

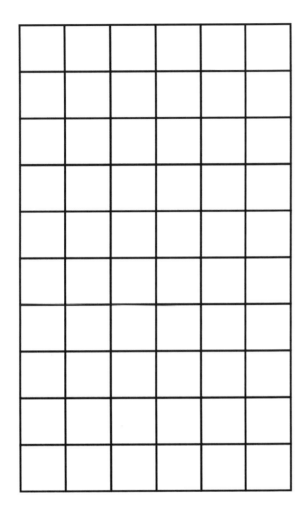

ALL FIRED UP

AWKWARD SILENCES

ACCEDES

CREAMY ALTERNATIVE

BY FAR

ADOPTS

GRANDFATHER TIMERS

PARK ACTIVITY

AT THE TABLE

AMOUNTS BEING BET

K	S
N	G

Z	E
E	S

L	Y
T	S

C	L
B	I

L	A
U	S

O	C
K	I

F	E
U	N

D	I
S	T

E	A
E	N

A	B
P	A

N	G
E	S

N	I
A	K

D	E
C	H

S	I
A	C

R	S
K	Y

#9

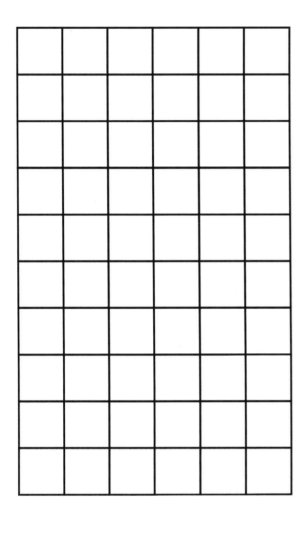

CONTRACT VIOLATION

BY FAR

ADOPTABLE ANIMALS

BLACKMAIL

ACQUIESCES

A BIG FAN

BUNDLE

CERTAIN DRESS CODE

BANGED UP A BIT

HIT A HIGH BALL

C	H	R	C	R	E
L	Y	S	U	O	W

A	G	S	T		
B	L	E	X		

E	S	D	E	B	R
E	R	L	O	E	A

P	A	E	D		
C	A	E	D		

Y	S	R	A	E	L
R	T	T	O	A	L

E	A	N	T		
S	I	F	T		

#10

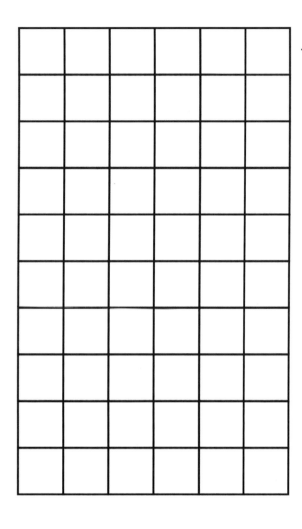

DEPARTED

BANDS OF INTRIGUE

BY PHYSICAL MEANS

A PERSIAN MARKET.

BLEMISH

FAVORED A FOOT

CAREER SOLDIERS

ARGUE

ACE

ASK FOR MORE TIME

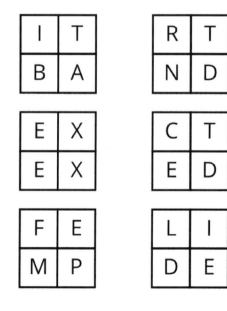

P	E
T	E

D	I
Z	A

B	O
B	A

I	T
B	A

R	T
N	D

F	E
B	A

L	Y
A	R

E	D
L	S

E	X
E	X

C	T
E	D

D	E
L	I

R	S
T	E

E	X
C	A

F	E
M	P

L	I
D	E

#11

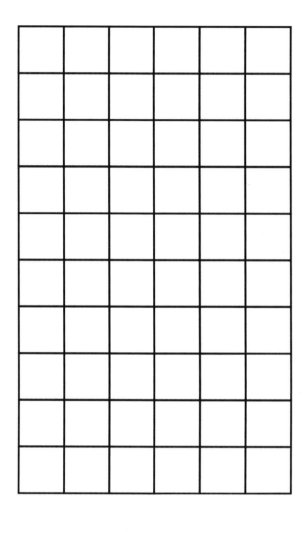

BAIT BUYER

BRIGHTNESS

ASLEEP NO MORE

BARK BOATS

DECKED OUT

BEAT IT

CARRIED OFF

BOTTLE-FED TYKES

"CAUGHT YOU!"

ADJUSTS, AS A HEM

O	T
B	I

P	P
N	I

O	K
N	O

E	D
R	S

E	R
S	H

D	A
V	A

B	U
A	L

G	L
S	T

A	W
C	A

L	O
B	A

S	T
T	E

A	N
L	U

E	D
E	S

E	N
E	S

E	R
E	R

#12

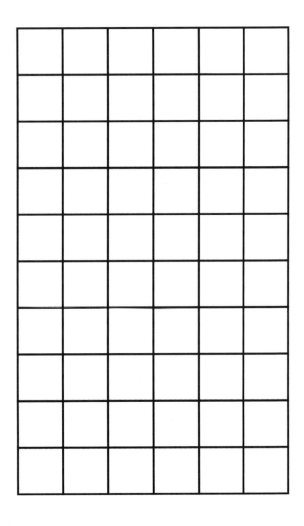

HIT A HIGH BALL

CHECKED FOR PRINTS

COMPLAIN

BOOT BLEMISHES

AMAZE

ANIMATED

EVEN MORE PROFOUND

APPLIES COLOR

AROMA SOURCE

BOOK JACKET BITS

B	O
B	O

L	O
D	U

K	E
U	R

E	R
T	S

M	O
U	F

B	E
S	C

L	E
C	Y

E	D
E	D

G	G
U	N

D	E
P	A

A	N
F	S

F	T
S	T

E	P
I	N

B	A
B	L

R	Y
B	S

#13

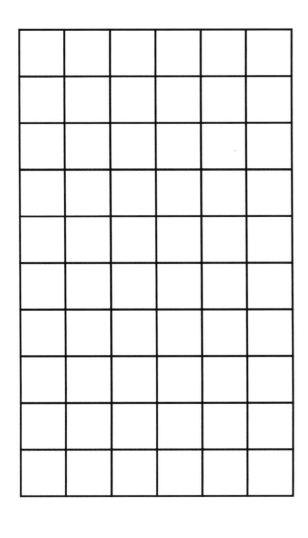

"BUCKING" HORSE

AMULETS.

AGILE

DABBED AT

AUTO REPAIR PERK

ATE LIKE A BIRD

BLATHER ON

ANGRY FROWNS

AMATEURISH ARTIST

CALMS DOWN

L	O
P	E

B	B
O	W

E	R
E	D

U	B
I	L

B	R
C	H

A	N
C	K

E	R
L	S

M	B
T	T

C	O
M	S

D	A
C	H

L	I
P	A

L	E
L	S

O	N
A	R

B	A
S	C

E	R
E	D

#14

BIG BOARD LISTINGS

ASSOCIATES

BLIZZARD BUILDUPS

BEST OF THE BEST

A COLOR BLUE

ARGUE FOR

DIDN'T HOLD WATER

ACCURSED

BIG CHEESES

ASSEMBLY RULES

S	T
A	L

T	S
X	E

O	C
L	I

I	F
L	U

K	S
E	S

B	O
B	Y

A	K
O	M

E	D
N	D

B	B
F	E

E	S
W	S

C	O
D	E

L	E
D	O

S	S
L	A

D	R
D	E

E	D
E	D

#15

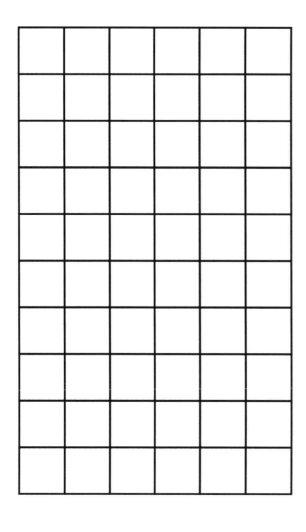

IN WAIT

AMULETS.

ALCHEMIC MIXTURE

ADDS A RIDER TO

RODE A BIKE

ACT INTRODUCERS

PLAY SLOWLY

CARRY AWAY

BIG DIPPERS

CLOSE

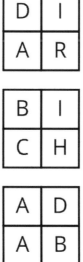
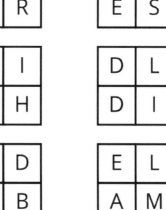

I	O
C	T

C	Y
E	M

D	I
A	R

E	D
E	S

E	S
N	G

L	A
E	N

I	R
D	S

B	I
C	H

D	L
D	I

I	X
E	N

C	L
C	E

A	G
D	U

A	D
A	B

E	L
A	M

N	G
M	S

#16

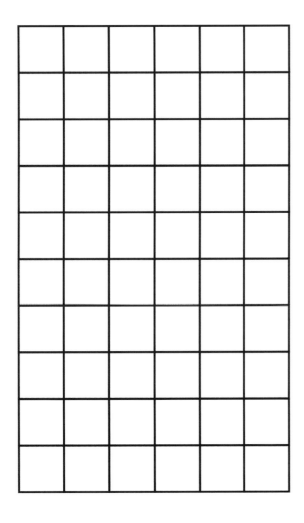

CARD TABLE PROJECT

A MONKEY'S UNCLE?

ALEUTIAN APPAREL

ABSTAINS FROM

BAKER'S OFFERING

"GRILLED" SANDWICH

BADGERED

ASLEEP NO MORE

BEACH PATRON

A PERSIAN MARKET.

I	T
O	K

B	A
B	A

E	D
E	N

P	A
C	H

S	T
E	E

A	W
O	N

R	Y
S	E

E	R
A	R

T	H
Z	A

B	A
A	W

G	S
B	O

A	S
D	S

J	I
B	A

P	A
A	V

R	K
O	I

#17

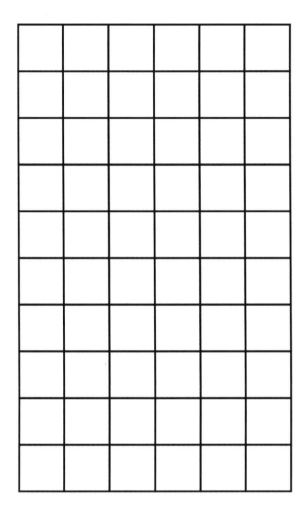

ATTENDANTS

CAREFULLY EXAMINED

"GET DOWN"

AMARETTO FLAVOR

OLYMPIC SPORT

A LA SCHOENBERG

ACTED IMPULSIVELY

ARRANGE FOR BATTLE

APPLIED BY PATS

CERTAIN DRESS CODE

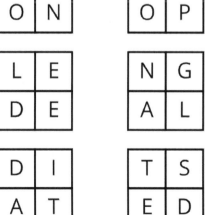

| V | A |
| S | C |

| D | A |
| C | A |

| A | P |
| P | L |

| V | I |
| O | N |

| L | E |
| O | P |

| I | E |
| N | D |

| O | G |
| M | O |

| B | B |
| S | U |

| L | E |
| D | E |

| N | G |
| A | L |

| E | D |
| O | Y |

| B | O |
| A | L |

| E | D |
| A | L |

| D | I |
| A | T |

| T | S |
| E | D |

#18

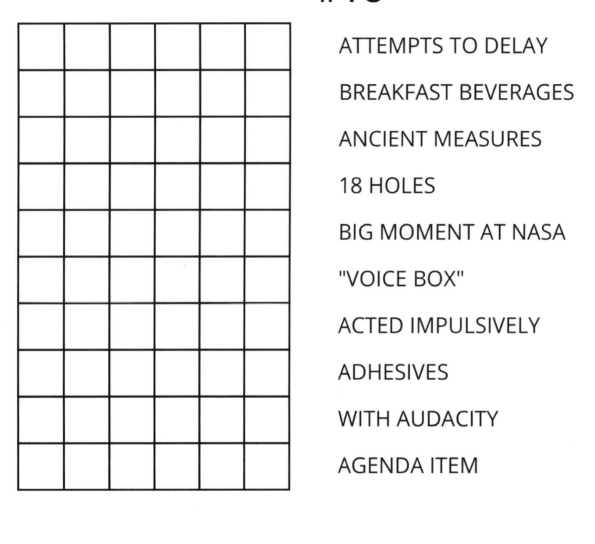

ATTEMPTS TO DELAY

BREAKFAST BEVERAGES

ANCIENT MEASURES

18 HOLES

BIG MOMENT AT NASA

"VOICE BOX"

ACTED IMPULSIVELY

ADHESIVES

WITH AUDACITY

AGENDA ITEM

L	E
P	A

U	N
R	Y

T	S
S	E

B	O
E	R

C	H
N	X

A	P
S	T

L	D
R	A

L	S
E	S

S	T
J	U

C	U
C	O

L	A
L	A

A	L
I	C

L	Y
N	D

B	I
U	R

E	D
E	S

#19

BAKERY GOODIES

ASTONISHED

CERTAIN SWITCH

BRING FORTH

FIGURES OUT

RUSSIAN GETAWAYS

CROP ATTACKER

BOX AT THE GYM?

ANGLE UNIT

ARRANGE FOR BATTLE

E	E
O	Y

E	R
I	T

C	R
D	A

H	T
E	R

D	I
E	L

S	C
A	M

A	C
C	H

I	G
C	K

E	S
E	D

D	E
D	E

G	R
P	L

M	M
I	C

K	S
A	S

O	N
A	Z

B	L
L	O

#20

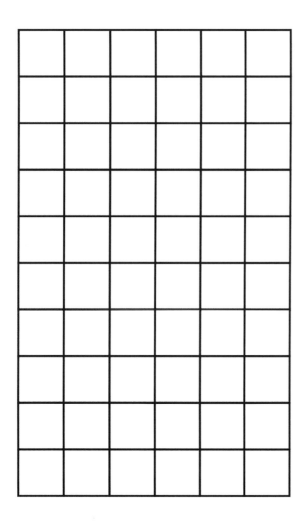

ALL ABOUT HORSES

ADORN.

ACCEPTED PRACTICE

ALMS SEEKER

TEAPOT COVERS

AWNING

BACKSPACE OVER

CELESTIAL

BURGER ADDITION

CARPENTER

T	E
A	L

C	A
J	O

U	I
T	I

S	T
G	G

O	M
A	R

Z	I
N	O

N	E
R	E

T	S
I	N

L	E
T	R

D	E
A	S

E	Q
A	T

C	O
C	A

U	P
E	R

E	S
P	Y

C	U
B	E

#21

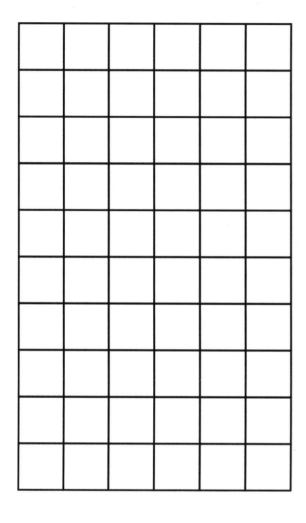

"CLOSE!"

A LA SCHOENBERG

ASCENDED

"I'M NOT ___ IT"

BATTED GENTLY

CARD TABLE PROJECT

"___ VISION"

DIDN'T HOLD WATER

ADD

ANIMALS

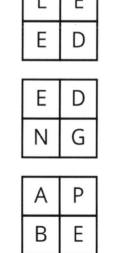

D	O
L	E

M	O
O	N

N	D
T	S

L	E
E	D

A	L
A	T

N	T
G	S

S	T
A	L

P	E
A	S

E	D
N	G

S	C
B	U

U	B
A	K

E	D
A	W

A	L
Y	I

A	P
B	E

B	U
J	I

#22

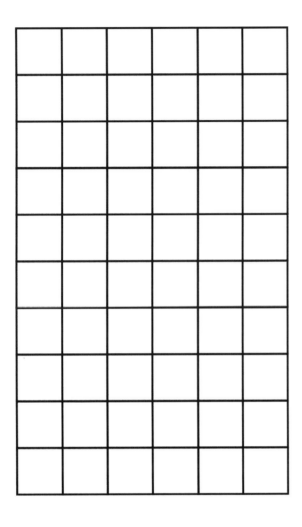

ENDURING

CARRIED ON

ARGUE

APPROACH A SUMMIT

BASEMENT FIXTURE

BRANCHES

AROSE, AS A STORM

CLEANS

BOOZEHOUNDS

CHEF APPAREL

I	L
U	G

E	W
O	U

E	R
H	S

D	R
A	P

B	I
A	S

U	N
R	O

B	O
B	O

C	K
C	E

N	G
E	D

E	R
N	D

K	S
N	S

B	R
S	C

E	D
R	S

P	I
S	T

C	O
L	A

#23

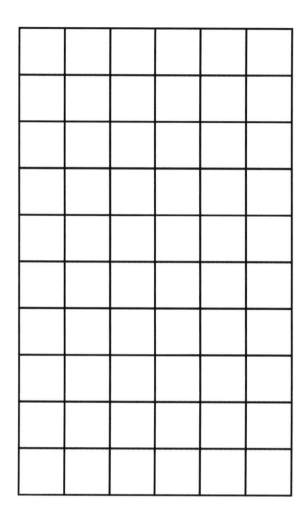

AGREEABLE SMELLS

ACKNOWLEDGE

BEANS OR CORN, E.G.

ASSIGNED A LABEL TO

DERIDES

TOOK MOVIE SHOTS.

BARK BOATS

WENT AGAINST

BARELY ADVANCES

ACCUSES

A	L
E	D

E	S
E	D

O	M
C	E

A	N
D	U

S	C
S	C

F	S
E	D

A	S
P	T

A	R
A	C

C	R
B	L

N	U
B	B

N	O
C	K

O	F
E	N

L	S
E	S

C	A
B	U

A	W
A	M

#24

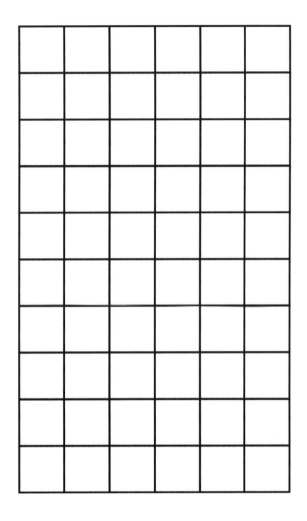

A COLOR BLUE

AIRPLANE WALKWAYS

"THE SCARLET ___"

DIDN'T HAVE

CASUAL JACKET

MADE A MEMO

CAST OFF

CONNECT

AUDUBON SUBJECTS

CAST OUT

D	I
L	I

A	Z
T	T

I	A
N	I

N	S
S	H

A	V
B	A

E	R
E	D

B	L
J	O

L	T
E	S

T	T
C	K

S	O
N	K

E	R
E	D

L	E
L	A

C	O
A	I

B	A
S	L

W	N
U	P

#1

B	R	I	B	E	S
C	A	S	U	A	L
D	I	P	O	L	E
L	A	C	K	E	D
L	A	S	T	L	Y
P	A	I	R	E	D
P	A	R	K	E	D
D	R	E	N	C	H
A	L	M	O	N	D
C	H	A	P	E	L

BUYOFFS

CERTAIN DRESS CODE

ANTENNA TYPE

DIDN'T HAVE

"IN CONCLUSION..."

ARRANGED IN TWOS

ACTED THE VALET

DELUGE

AMARETTO FLAVOR

"I DO" SETTING

#2

B	O	O	S	T	S
D	I	V	I	N	G
L	O	S	S	E	S
A	R	T	I	E	R
L	I	K	E	L	Y
B	A	K	I	N	G
B	R	I	D	A	L
B	O	W	M	A	N
B	U	C	K	E	D
E	D	I	B	L	E

ENCOURAGEMENTS

OLYMPIC SPORT

ACCOUNTING STATS

LESS TACKY

APPARENTLY SUITABLE

HOT

KIND OF GOWN

ARCHER

WENT AGAINST

ACCEPTABLE TO EAT

#3

V	A	C	A	T	E
J	O	K	E	R	S
A	N	N	U	L	S
P	E	N	N	E	D
C	R	E	E	P	S
B	R	E	W	E	D
J	O	B	B	E	R
S	T	O	O	P	S
D	O	R	M	E	R
B	O	U	N	T	Y

ABANDON

BOZOS

BLOTS OUT

AUTHORED

ADVANCES LIKE IVY

AROSE, AS A STORM

MIDDLEMAN.

BAD POSTURES

ATTIC OPENING

ABUNDANCE

#4

B	R	A	V	E	R
S	T	A	I	N	S
C	A	N	O	P	Y
A	L	I	G	N	S
D	E	F	I	N	E
S	T	R	A	I	T
B	E	A	C	O	N
B	A	N	N	E	R
C	A	V	I	A	R
P	E	D	A	L	S

LESS CHICKEN

ADDS COLOR TO

AWNING

ADJUSTS

CHARACTERIZE

BERING --

AID TO NAVIGATORS

AD FORM

BANQUET DELICACY

BICYCLE FEATURES

#5

L	O	G	J	A	M
L	A	S	T	L	Y
C	U	P	F	U	L
E	I	G	H	T	H
E	X	C	I	T	E
B	A	K	I	N	G
A	L	L	I	E	S
L	A	Y	O	U	T
S	T	A	K	E	S
C	A	D	G	E	R

BACKUP

"IN CONCLUSION..."

COFFEE MEASURE

BEFORE NINTH

AROUSE

HOT

ASSOCIATES

ARRANGEMENT

AMOUNTS BEING BET

FREE LOADER.

#6

B	O	Y	I	S	H
D	R	E	N	C	H
C	O	B	A	L	T
A	D	J	U	S	T
C	U	P	F	U	L
E	N	D	O	W	S
D	U	N	C	E	S
S	C	O	P	E	D
A	G	R	E	E	D
B	E	L	I	E	F

ENGAGINGLY INNOCEN

DELUGE

A COLOR BLUE

BE ACCOMMODATING

COFFEE MEASURE

BACKS FINANCIALLY

AIRHEADS

CAREFULLY EXAMINED

"AMEN!"

ACCEPTED DOCTRINE

#7

E	V	E	N	L	Y
C	O	I	N	E	D
B	U	R	E	A	U
L	O	C	K	E	R
D	R	U	N	K	S
L	O	D	G	E	R
A	U	D	I	T	S
C	E	M	E	N	T
C	L	I	M	A	X
D	U	S	T	E	D

FAIR WAY TO SHARE

CREATED OR INVENTED

AGENCY

BOX AT THE GYM?

BOOZEHOUNDS

BOARDER

ACCOUNTING JOBS

ADHESIVE SURFACE.

BIG FINISH

CHECKED FOR PRINTS

#8

A	B	L	A	Z	E
P	A	U	S	E	S
D	E	F	E	R	S
C	H	U	N	K	Y
E	A	S	I	L	Y
E	N	A	C	T	S
C	L	O	C	K	S
B	I	K	I	N	G
D	I	N	I	N	G
S	T	A	K	E	S

ALL FIRED UP

AWKWARD SILENCES

ACCEDES

CREAMY ALTERNATIVE

BY FAR

ADOPTS

GRANDFATHER TIMERS

PARK ACTIVITY

AT THE TABLE

AMOUNTS BEING BET

#9

B	R	E	A	C	H
E	A	S	I	L	Y
S	T	R	A	Y	S
E	X	T	O	R	T
A	G	R	E	E	S
B	L	O	W	E	R
P	A	R	C	E	L
C	A	S	U	A	L
D	E	N	T	E	D
L	O	F	T	E	D

CONTRACT VIOLATION

BY FAR

ADOPTABLE ANIMALS

BLACKMAIL

ACQUIESCES

A BIG FAN

BUNDLE

CERTAIN DRESS CODE

BANGED UP A BIT

HIT A HIGH BALL

#10

E	X	I	T	E	D
C	A	B	A	L	S
B	O	D	I	L	Y
B	A	Z	A	A	R
D	E	F	E	C	T
L	I	M	P	E	D
L	I	F	E	R	S
D	E	B	A	T	E
E	X	P	E	R	T
E	X	T	E	N	D

DEPARTED

BANDS OF INTRIGUE

BY PHYSICAL MEANS

A PERSIAN MARKET.

BLEMISH

FAVORED A FOOT

CAREER SOLDIERS

ARGUE

ACE

ASK FOR MORE TIME

#11

A	N	G	L	E	R
L	U	S	T	E	R
A	W	O	K	E	N
C	A	N	O	E	S
D	A	P	P	E	R
V	A	N	I	S	H
L	O	O	T	E	D
B	A	B	I	E	S
B	U	S	T	E	D
A	L	T	E	R	S

BAIT BUYER

BRIGHTNESS

ASLEEP NO MORE

BARK BOATS

DECKED OUT

BEAT IT

CARRIED OFF

BOTTLE-FED TYKES

"CAUGHT YOU!"

ADJUSTS, AS A HEM

#12

L	O	F	T	E	D
D	U	S	T	E	D
B	E	M	O	A	N
S	C	U	F	F	S
B	O	G	G	L	E
B	O	U	N	C	Y
D	E	E	P	E	R
P	A	I	N	T	S
B	A	K	E	R	Y
B	L	U	R	B	S

HIT A HIGH BALL

CHECKED FOR PRINTS

COMPLAIN

BOOT BLEMISHES

AMAZE

ANIMATED

EVEN MORE PROFOUND

APPLIES COLOR

AROMA SOURCE

BOOK JACKET BITS

#13

B	R	O	N	C	O
C	H	A	R	M	S
L	I	M	B	E	R
P	A	T	T	E	D
L	O	A	N	E	R
P	E	C	K	E	D
B	A	B	B	L	E
S	C	O	W	L	S
D	A	U	B	E	R
C	H	I	L	L	S

"BUCKING" HORSE

AMULETS.

AGILE

DABBED AT

AUTO REPAIR PERK

ATE LIKE A BIRD

BLATHER ON

ANGRY FROWNS

AMATEURISH ARTIST

CALMS DOWN

#14

S	T	O	C	K	S
A	L	L	I	E	S
D	R	I	F	T	S
D	E	L	U	X	E
C	O	B	B	E	D
D	E	F	E	N	D
L	E	A	K	E	D
D	O	O	M	E	D
B	O	S	S	E	S
B	Y	L	A	W	S

BIG BOARD LISTINGS

ASSOCIATES

BLIZZARD BUILDUPS

BEST OF THE BEST

A COLOR BLUE

ARGUE FOR

DIDN'T HOLD WATER

ACCURSED

BIG CHEESES

ASSEMBLY RULES

#15

B	I	D	I	N	G
C	H	A	R	M	S
E	L	I	X	I	R
A	M	E	N	D	S
C	Y	C	L	E	D
E	M	C	E	E	S
A	D	A	G	I	O
A	B	D	U	C	T
L	A	D	L	E	S
E	N	D	I	N	G

IN WAIT

AMULETS.

ALCHEMIC MIXTURE

ADDS A RIDER TO

RODE A BIKE

ACT INTRODUCERS

PLAY SLOWLY

CARRY AWAY

BIG DIPPERS

CLOSE

#16

J	I	G	S	A	W
B	A	B	O	O	N
P	A	R	K	A	S
A	V	O	I	D	S
P	A	S	T	R	Y
C	H	E	E	S	E
B	A	I	T	E	D
A	W	O	K	E	N
B	A	T	H	E	R
B	A	Z	A	A	R

CARD TABLE PROJECT

A MONKEY'S UNCLE?

ALEUTIAN APPAREL

ABSTAINS FROM

BAKER'S OFFERING

"GRILLED" SANDWICH

BADGERED

ASLEEP NO MORE

BEACH PATRON

A PERSIAN MARKET.

#17

V	A	L	E	T	S
S	C	O	P	E	D
B	O	O	G	I	E
A	L	M	O	N	D
A	D	I	V	I	N	G
A	T	O	N	A	L
L	E	A	P	E	D
D	E	P	L	O	Y
D	A	B	B	E	D
C	A	S	U	A	L

ATTENDANTS
CAREFULLY EXAMINED
"GET DOWN"
AMARETTO FLAVOR
OLYMPIC SPORT
A LA SCHOENBERG
ACTED IMPULSIVELY
ARRANGE FOR BATTLE
APPLIED BY PATS
CERTAIN DRESS CODE

#18

S	T	A	L	L	S
J	U	I	C	E	S
C	U	B	I	T	S
C	O	U	R	S	E
L	A	U	N	C	H
L	A	R	Y	N	X
L	E	A	P	E	D
P	A	S	T	E	S
B	O	L	D	L	Y
E	R	R	A	N	D

ATTEMPTS TO DELAY
BREAKFAST BEVERAGES
ANCIENT MEASURES
18 HOLES
BIG MOMENT AT NASA
"VOICE BOX"
ACTED IMPULSIVELY
ADHESIVES
WITH AUDACITY
AGENDA ITEM

#19

S	C	O	N	E	S
A	M	A	Z	E	D
D	I	M	M	E	R
E	L	I	C	I	T
C	R	A	C	K	S
D	A	C	H	A	S
B	L	I	G	H	T
L	O	C	K	E	R
D	E	G	R	E	E
D	E	P	L	O	Y

BAKERY GOODIES
ASTONISHED
CERTAIN SWITCH
BRING FORTH
FIGURES OUT
RUSSIAN GETAWAYS
CROP ATTACKER
BOX AT THE GYM?
ANGLE UNIT
ARRANGE FOR BATTLE

#20

E	Q	U	I	N	E
A	T	T	I	R	E
C	U	S	T	O	M
B	E	G	G	A	R
C	O	Z	I	E	S
C	A	N	O	P	Y
D	E	L	E	T	E
A	S	T	R	A	L
C	A	T	S	U	P
J	O	I	N	E	R

ALL ABOUT HORSES
ADORN.
ACCEPTED PRACTICE
ALMS SEEKER
TEAPOT COVERS
AWNING
BACKSPACE OVER
CELESTIAL
BURGER ADDITION
CARPENTER

#21

A	L	M	O	S	T
A	T	O	N	A	L
S	C	A	L	E	D
B	U	Y	I	N	G
B	U	N	T	E	D
J	I	G	S	A	W
D	O	U	B	L	E
L	E	A	K	E	D
A	P	P	E	N	D
B	E	A	S	T	S

"CLOSE!"
A LA SCHOENBERG
ASCENDED
"I'M NOT ___ IT"
BATTED GENTLY
CARD TABLE PROJECT
"___ VISION"
DIDN'T HOLD WATER
ADD
ANIMALS

#22

C	O	P	I	N	G
L	A	S	T	E	D
B	I	C	K	E	R
A	S	C	E	N	D
B	O	I	L	E	R
B	O	U	G	H	S
B	R	E	W	E	D
S	C	O	U	R	S
D	R	U	N	K	S
A	P	R	O	N	S

ENDURING
CARRIED ON
ARGUE
APPROACH A SUMMIT
BASEMENT FIXTURE
BRANCHES
AROSE, AS A STORM
CLEANS
BOOZEHOUNDS
CHEF APPAREL

#23

A	R	O	M	A	S
A	C	C	E	P	T
A	N	N	U	A	L
D	U	B	B	E	D
S	C	O	F	F	S
S	C	E	N	E	D
C	A	N	O	E	S
B	U	C	K	E	D
C	R	A	W	L	S
B	L	A	M	E	S

AGREEABLE SMELLS
ACKNOWLEDGE
BEANS OR CORN, E.G.
ASSIGNED A LABEL TO
DERIDES
TOOK MOVIE SHOTS.
BARK BOATS
WENT AGAINST
BARELY ADVANCES
ACCUSES

#24

C	O	B	A	L	T
A	I	S	L	E	S
L	E	T	T	E	R
L	A	C	K	E	D
B	L	A	Z	E	R
J	O	T	T	E	D
D	I	S	O	W	N
L	I	N	K	U	P
A	V	I	A	N	S
B	A	N	I	S	H

A COLOR BLUE
AIRPLANE WALKWAYS
"THE SCARLET ___"
DIDN'T HAVE
CASUAL JACKET
MADE A MEMO
CAST OFF
CONNECT
AUDUBON SUBJECTS
CAST OUT

Sudoku

To complete a sudoku puzzle, a 9 by 9 grid must be filled in with numbers from 1 to 9, with each number appearing exactly once within each grid or row.

First rule: Use only the digits 1 through 9 and do not repeat them across rows, columns, and each inner 3 by 3 grid.

Second rule: Don't try to guess. If you put in a wrong number, the rest of the problem will remain unanswered until you get it right.

Finally, use process of elimination. It is possible to fill in the grid by using the existing numbers.

	3			1			4	
					5			
	9			5		2		3
9		6			3	8	5	
		5			4		6	
7			5		9	3	2	4
	8	9		2	1			
2			6		8		3	9
				9				

Puzzle #1

					5		9	2
6	4						5	
	8			3		1		4
9		6	3			7	2	
		8						9
		1		7		5		
				5	3			7
5			2	6	8	9	4	
3			4		7		1	

Puzzle #2

1					5		7	3
6	2							
		3		8				
			3					
4	3		9		7	6	1	2
5	6	2	4		8			
2				7	4	3		
		1	2	3			5	
		4				2		8

Puzzle #3

	7		4			2		
		4	2			3	7	8
			5		3			
						5		9
5		1			6	4		
	6		3	5			1	2
		7	6	3				1
				2		9		
					5	6		

Puzzle #4

7			2	8			3	4
	1			3	9			8
		3	5	6				
1					3	5		
	9		4			7	2	
	3	2		5				9
5							7	
						3		5
	2	7	8	4	5			

Puzzle #5

9	7			3	1	8		
	5		7	2	6	3		1
	6			4				
	8				7	6		3
4				6	2		1	
5						2		8
	9		2	7	3	4	8	
							3	
					5	9		

Puzzle #6

5	4	2				1		6
				3			4	
3	7			4			8	
6		8		1	3		2	7
		4	7		6	9		3
2	8				9	7	1	
	9				8			2
			4		5			

Puzzle #7

		2		8		6		
			2				8	
1			5	4	7		9	
8	4			6			3	
9	5		1					
						7	1	
				7				
7	8		9	2		3	4	1
	3	5					2	

Puzzle #8

	3			1			4	
						5		
	9			5		2		3
9		6			3	8	5	
		5			4		6	
7			5		9	3	2	4
	8	9		2	1			
2			6		8		3	9
				9				

Puzzle #9

						4	8	
3		4		7				9
2		9		1			5	7
9	1	3	6					
		2	1	5				3
	5		2				1	4
			8			7		
		8		4			2	1
1		7			9			

Puzzle #10

	4			3	7		6	
	2		9	1				
		1				5		2
	9				4			
2		4	6	5			3	
			7			2	4	8
3		2					5	
1		6		8	3			7
							8	3

Puzzle #11

		7	1					5
4		1		5				9
2		3			7		1	
			7	8		6	3	1
3		9			6			
					2		7	
9					1		4	2
		2			5	1	6	3
1			3	2		5		

Puzzle #12

	1		9	7		6	5	
	9	8					3	4
		5				2		
9			5	6				
5						9		
	6				2			7
	5	1				3	7	
8		9	6			1	4	
			3		1	8	9	

Puzzle #13

5		4			9	8		
2			3		5	4		7
			6				9	1
	1							
			9	1	2		4	5
4		9	8			2	1	
				5			8	
	8							2
3			7	9			5	

Puzzle #14

3			7		8		9	
		6	2		5	1		8
8			1	4				5
	9						8	
			5			9		7
	3	1		8		2		
			4	7				
		3	8				4	
	7			1	6		5	

Puzzle #15

					7	1	2	
	9		1	4	6			
1				5	3			4
	3			7			6	
5								
6			5		8		9	2
	2	1				3		
9		7			1			8
	6	5	4		9		1	

Puzzle #16

1			7	2				6
			4		1			9
8	2	4	3	9			7	
	9	2		7	3			8
	3	8			4		1	2
							3	
			5		7	6		
9							8	3
6	1		8			7	2	

Puzzle #17

9	1				5		3	2
	8				2			7
	4	7	6	3	8			
	2	8	3	4		5		1
						6		
6		9			7	3		4
	9	5						
		1	7		3	2	4	
							8	

Puzzle #18

	1					3		
	5	2			1			8
	7	3	4					
			6		2	9	3	5
	6	5	3				7	
3		7			8	6		
2				9		7		
	9				7		6	
		1	2	8				

Puzzle #19

5				6	7	2		
			4					
2				9	3	1	7	
			3	4	6	7		
		3	7			4		2
		6		5	2		1	8
		1		7	5	9		
3		5		1				
4		8	2					1

Puzzle #20

		3		9				6
8						3	7	
	5	1	4	7			2	8
		7	2		4	6	3	
	3						9	
	1		3					
9			7	4		5	8	
		4	8				6	9
		5			6			2

Puzzle #1

1	7	3	8	4	5	6	9	2
6	4	9	7	2	1	3	5	8
2	8	5	6	3	9	1	7	4
9	5	6	3	8	4	7	2	1
7	2	8	5	1	6	4	3	9
4	3	1	9	7	2	5	8	6
8	9	4	1	5	3	2	6	7
5	1	7	2	6	8	9	4	3
3	6	2	4	9	7	8	1	5

Puzzle #2

1	8	9	6	2	5	4	7	3
6	2	5	7	4	3	1	8	9
7	4	3	1	8	9	5	2	6
9	1	7	3	6	2	8	4	5
4	3	8	9	5	7	6	1	2
5	6	2	4	1	8	9	3	7
2	5	6	8	7	4	3	9	1
8	9	1	2	3	6	7	5	4
3	7	4	5	9	1	2	6	8

Puzzle #3

3	7	6	4	8	1	2	9	5
1	5	4	2	6	9	3	7	8
9	8	2	5	7	3	1	4	6
7	3	8	1	4	2	5	6	9
5	2	1	7	9	6	4	8	3
4	6	9	3	5	8	7	1	2
2	9	7	6	3	4	8	5	1
6	1	5	8	2	7	9	3	4
8	4	3	9	1	5	6	2	7

Puzzle #4

7	5	9	2	8	1	6	3	4
4	1	6	7	3	9	2	5	8
2	8	3	5	6	4	1	9	7
1	7	4	9	2	3	5	8	6
6	9	5	4	1	8	7	2	3
8	3	2	6	5	7	4	1	9
5	4	1	3	9	6	8	7	2
9	6	8	1	7	2	3	4	5
3	2	7	8	4	5	9	6	1

Puzzle #5

9	7	2	5	3	1	8	6	4
8	5	4	7	2	6	3	9	1
1	6	3	9	4	8	7	5	2
2	8	9	1	5	7	6	4	3
4	3	7	8	6	2	5	1	9
5	1	6	3	9	4	2	7	8
6	9	1	2	7	3	4	8	5
7	2	5	4	8	9	1	3	6
3	4	8	6	1	5	9	2	7

Puzzle #6

8	3	1	6	5	4	2	7	9
5	4	2	8	9	7	1	3	6
9	6	7	2	3	1	8	4	5
3	7	9	5	4	2	6	8	1
6	5	8	9	1	3	4	2	7
1	2	4	7	8	6	9	5	3
2	8	5	3	6	9	7	1	4
4	9	3	1	7	8	5	6	2
7	1	6	4	2	5	3	9	8

Puzzle #7

5	9	2	3	8	1	6	7	4
3	7	4	2	9	6	1	8	5
1	6	8	5	4	7	2	9	3
8	4	1	7	6	9	5	3	2
9	5	7	1	3	2	4	6	8
6	2	3	8	5	4	7	1	9
2	1	9	4	7	3	8	5	6
7	8	6	9	2	5	3	4	1
4	3	5	6	1	8	9	2	7

Puzzle #8

5	3	2	9	1	6	7	4	8
8	7	1	4	3	2	5	9	6
6	9	4	8	5	7	2	1	3
9	4	6	2	7	3	8	5	1
3	2	5	1	8	4	9	6	7
7	1	8	5	6	9	3	2	4
4	8	9	3	2	1	6	7	5
2	5	7	6	4	8	1	3	9
1	6	3	7	9	5	4	8	2

Puzzle #9

5	7	1	9	3	6	4	8	2
3	8	4	5	7	2	1	6	9
2	6	9	4	1	8	3	5	7
9	1	3	6	8	4	2	7	5
8	4	2	1	5	7	6	9	3
7	5	6	2	9	3	8	1	4
4	9	5	8	2	1	7	3	6
6	3	8	7	4	5	9	2	1
1	2	7	3	6	9	5	4	8

Puzzle #10

9	4	5	2	3	7	8	6	1
6	2	8	9	1	5	3	7	4
7	3	1	8	4	6	5	9	2
8	9	7	3	2	4	6	1	5
2	1	4	6	5	8	7	3	9
5	6	3	7	9	1	2	4	8
3	8	2	1	7	9	4	5	6
1	5	6	4	8	3	9	2	7
4	7	9	5	6	2	1	8	3

Puzzle #11

8	9	7	1	6	4	3	2	5
4	6	1	2	5	3	7	8	9
2	5	3	8	9	7	4	1	6
5	2	4	7	8	9	6	3	1
3	7	9	4	1	6	2	5	8
6	1	8	5	3	2	9	7	4
9	3	5	6	7	1	8	4	2
7	8	2	9	4	5	1	6	3
1	4	6	3	2	8	5	9	7

Puzzle #12

3	1	2	9	7	4	6	5	8
6	9	8	1	2	5	7	3	4
7	4	5	8	3	6	2	1	9
9	8	7	5	6	3	4	2	1
5	2	4	7	1	8	9	6	3
1	6	3	4	9	2	5	8	7
4	5	1	2	8	9	3	7	6
8	3	9	6	5	7	1	4	2
2	7	6	3	4	1	8	9	5

Puzzle #13

5	6	4	1	7	9	8	2	3
2	9	1	3	8	5	4	6	7
8	7	3	6	2	4	5	9	1
7	1	2	5	4	6	9	3	8
6	3	8	9	1	2	7	4	5
4	5	9	8	3	7	2	1	6
1	4	7	2	5	3	6	8	9
9	8	5	4	6	1	3	7	2
3	2	6	7	9	8	1	5	4

Puzzle #14

3	1	5	7	6	8	4	9	2
7	4	6	2	9	5	1	3	8
8	2	9	1	4	3	6	7	5
4	9	7	6	2	1	5	8	3
6	8	2	5	3	4	9	1	7
5	3	1	9	8	7	2	6	4
1	5	8	4	7	9	3	2	6
9	6	3	8	5	2	7	4	1
2	7	4	3	1	6	8	5	9

Puzzle #15

4	5	3	8	9	7	1	2	6
7	9	2	1	4	6	8	3	5
1	8	6	2	5	3	9	7	4
2	3	8	9	7	4	5	6	1
5	7	9	6	1	2	4	8	3
6	1	4	5	3	8	7	9	2
8	2	1	7	6	5	3	4	9
9	4	7	3	2	1	6	5	8
3	6	5	4	8	9	2	1	7

Puzzle #16

1	5	9	7	2	8	3	4	6
3	7	6	4	5	1	2	8	9
8	2	4	3	9	6	1	7	5
5	9	2	1	7	3	4	6	8
7	3	8	9	6	4	5	1	2
4	6	1	2	8	5	9	3	7
2	8	3	5	4	7	6	9	1
9	4	7	6	1	2	8	5	3
6	1	5	8	3	9	7	2	4

Puzzle #17

9	1	6	4	7	5	8	3	2
5	8	3	9	1	2	4	6	7
2	4	7	6	3	8	1	5	9
7	2	8	3	4	6	5	9	1
1	3	4	2	5	9	6	7	8
6	5	9	1	8	7	3	2	4
3	9	5	8	2	4	7	1	6
8	6	1	7	9	3	2	4	5
4	7	2	5	6	1	9	8	3

Puzzle #18

4	1	9	8	6	5	3	2	7
6	5	2	7	3	1	4	9	8
8	7	3	4	2	9	1	5	6
1	8	4	6	7	2	9	3	5
9	6	5	3	1	4	8	7	2
3	2	7	9	5	8	6	1	4
2	4	6	5	9	3	7	8	1
5	9	8	1	4	7	2	6	3
7	3	1	2	8	6	5	4	9

Puzzle #19

5	3	9	1	6	7	2	8	4
1	6	7	4	2	8	5	3	9
2	8	4	5	9	3	1	7	6
8	1	2	3	4	6	7	9	5
9	5	3	7	8	1	4	6	2
7	4	6	9	5	2	3	1	8
6	2	1	8	7	5	9	4	3
3	9	5	6	1	4	8	2	7
4	7	8	2	3	9	6	5	1

Puzzle #20

7	2	3	5	9	8	4	1	6
8	4	9	6	1	2	3	7	5
6	5	1	4	7	3	9	2	8
5	9	7	2	8	4	6	3	1
2	3	6	1	5	7	8	9	4
4	1	8	3	6	9	2	5	7
9	6	2	7	4	1	5	8	3
3	7	4	8	2	5	1	6	9
1	8	5	9	3	6	7	4	2

Nonograms

Do you know what a nonogram is?

Nonograms are a type of logic puzzle in which the number of sides determines the color or absence of a certain cell in a grid.

The numbers in this type of problem are representations of the total number of continuous rows of squares across the board.

When you see the notation "2 1," it signifies that there is a group of two and a group of one, with at minimum one empty square in between.

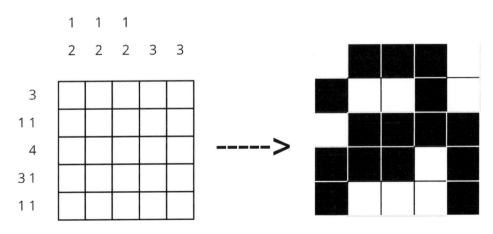

#1

Column clues:
```
            1   1
    1   2   1       2   2       1   1   1
    2   1   1   3   2   1   3   1   1   2
    1   1   2   1   1   1   3   1   2   1
```

Row clues:
- 1 2 3
- 1 2 1
- 8
- 1 1
- 2 1 1 1
- 1 1 1 2 1
- 1 1
- 1 2
- 3 1
- 3 1

#2

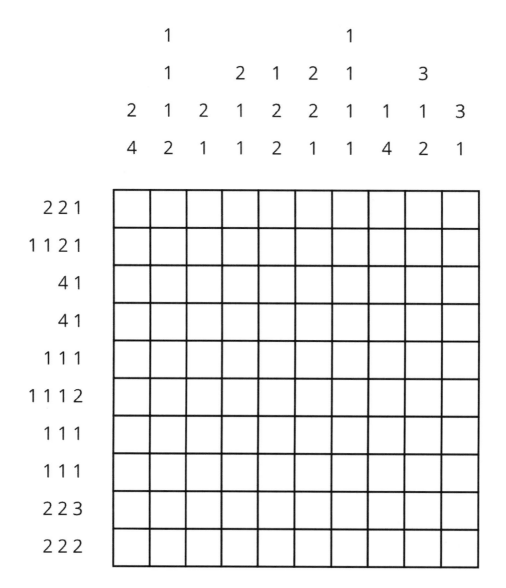

#3

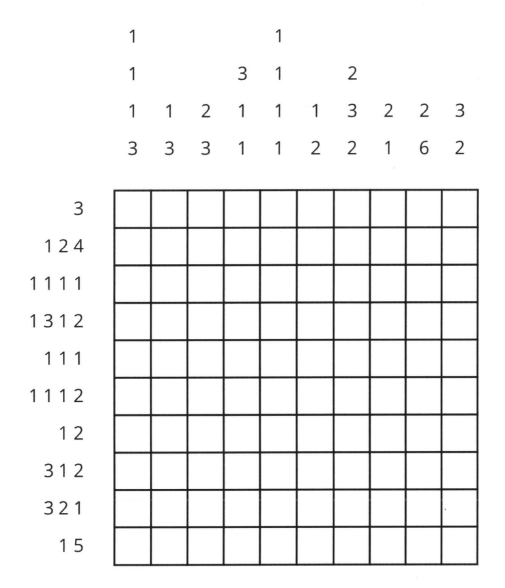

#4

						1				
		1		4	1	1	1		5	
	4	2	1	1	2	1	1	1	1	1
	3	2	4	2	2	2	2	1	1	3
3										
4 1										
1 4 1										
5 1										
3 3										
2 2 1										
1 1 1										
1 1 2										
2 4 1										
1 2 3										

#5

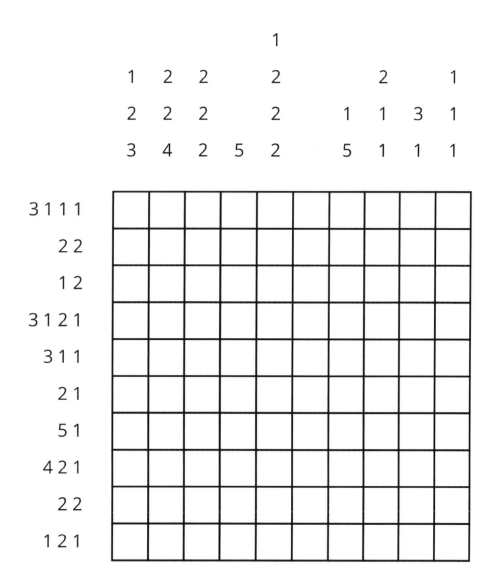

#6

<table>
<tr><td></td><td>1</td><td></td><td></td><td></td><td>1</td><td></td><td></td><td></td><td></td></tr>
<tr><td>2</td><td>1</td><td>2</td><td>1</td><td></td><td>1</td><td></td><td></td><td></td><td>2</td></tr>
<tr><td>1</td><td>3</td><td>1</td><td>2</td><td>4</td><td>2</td><td></td><td>2</td><td>3</td><td>1</td></tr>
<tr><td>1</td><td>3</td><td>3</td><td>3</td><td>1</td><td>1</td><td>6</td><td>2</td><td>1</td><td>1</td></tr>
</table>

Row clues:
- 2 1 2
- 1 1
- 7 2
- 5 3
- 1 6
- 1 3
- 1 1
- 3 1 1
- 5 1
- 2 2

#7

		1	1							
	4	1	1			2				1
	2	1	1	4	5	1	4		3	1
	1	1	1	2	1	1	3	5	1	1
2 1										
1 2 4										
1 6										
2 6										
1 3 2 1										
1										
1 1 2 1										
2 1 1										
1 2 1										
3 1										

#8

		1		1					2	
		1	1	1		1		1	1	
	3	1	1	1	1	1	5	3	1	
	2	2	3	1	1	1	2	2	3	1

1 1 1										
1 1 1 1										
1 1 3										
4 4										
3										
5 1										
1 2										
2 1										
1 1 4										
1 1 1 2										

#9

Column clues:

	2					1				
	1			1		1	1		1	
	2	1	2	4	5	2	4	6	5	3
	2	2	2	1	2	1	1	2	1	1

Row clues:

1 1 1 2
1 1 1 2 1
1 1 1 1
1 7
1 2 3
1 6
1 1 2 1
1 1 3
5 2
1 1 1 1

#10

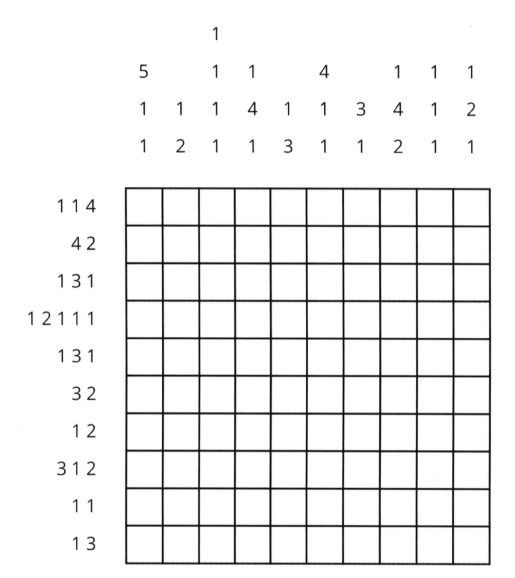

#11

Column clues (left to right):
- 3 1
- 1 3 1 1
- 2 2
- 1 1 1 1
- 2 1 1
- 1 2
- 3 2 2
- 1 2 1
- 2 1 1
- 1 1

Row clues (top to bottom):
- 1
- 6 1
- 1 1 1 1
- 1 2 1
- 1 1
- 2 2 1
- 1 1 2 1
- 4 1 1
- 1 1
- 2 2 1 1

#12

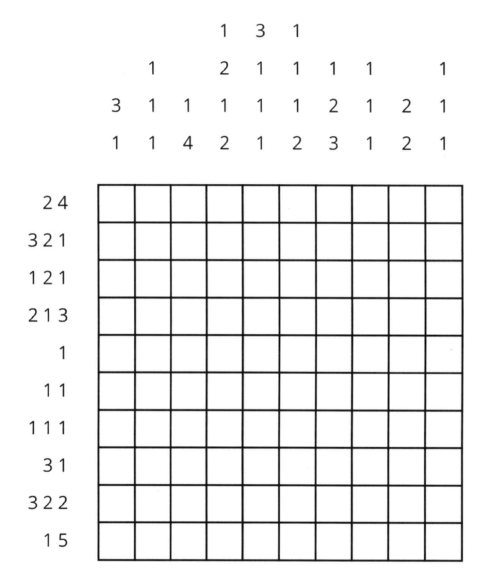

#13

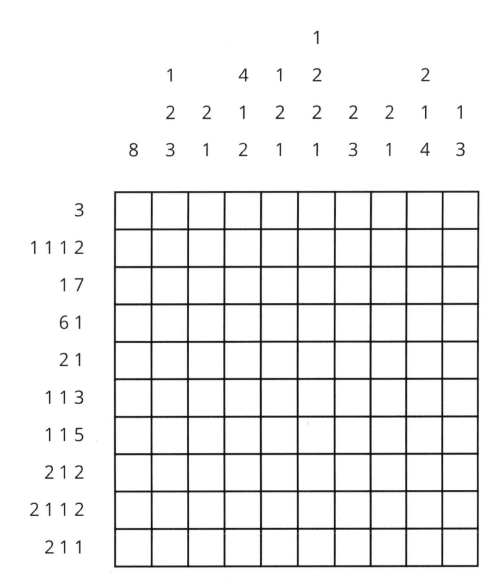

#14

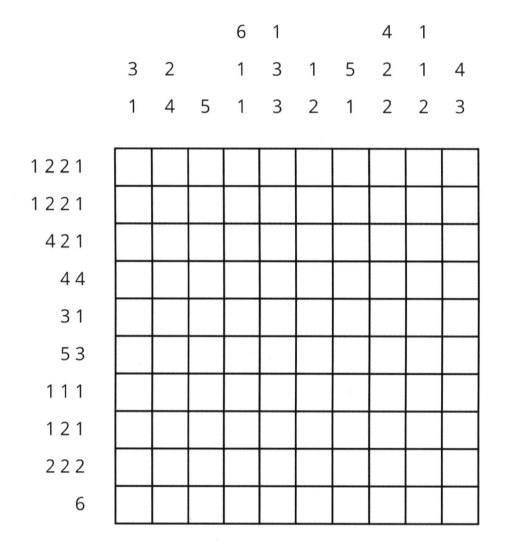

#15

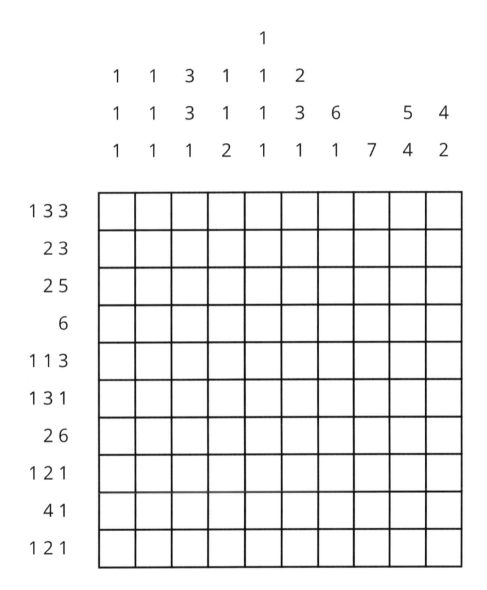

#16

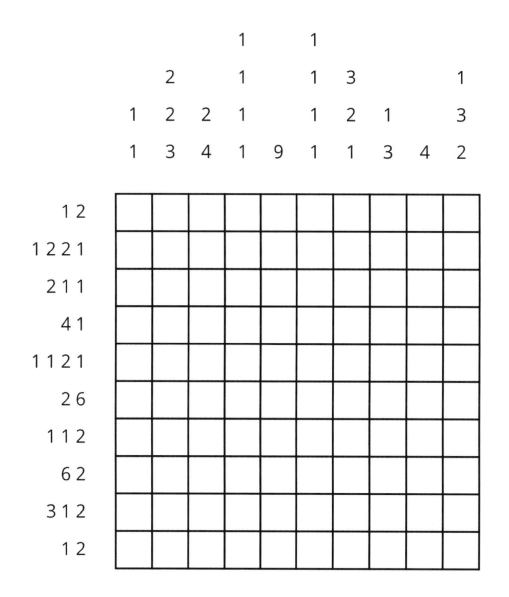

#17

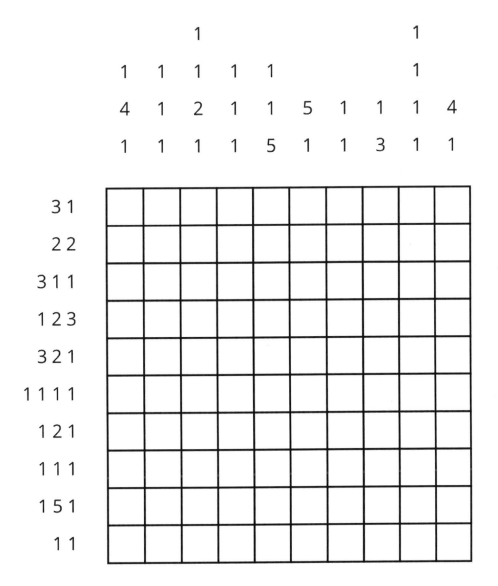

#18

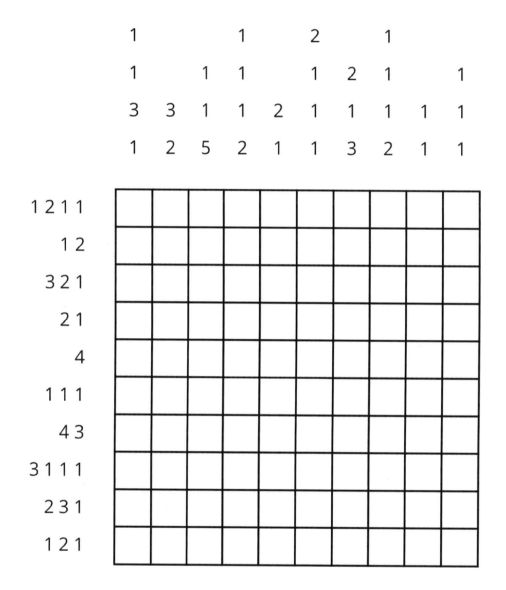

#19

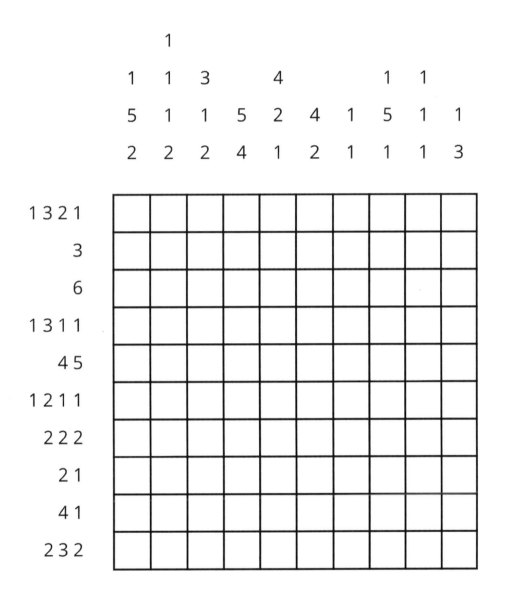

#20

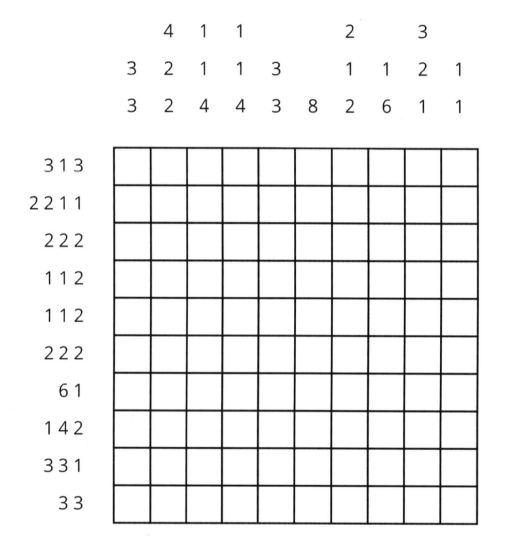

#1

#2

#3

#4

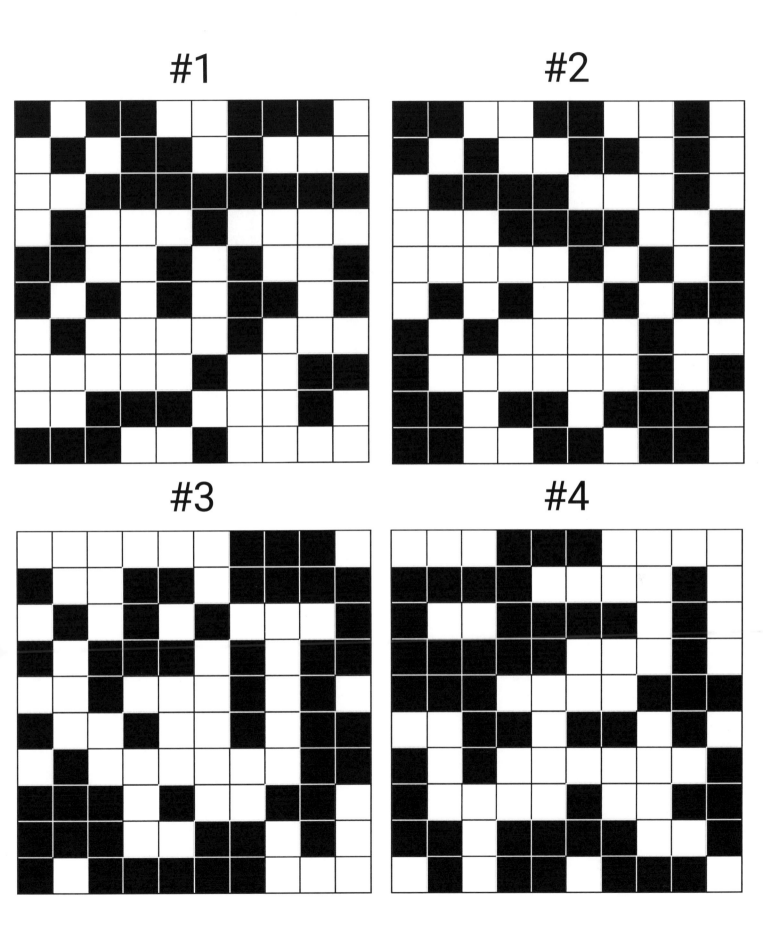

91

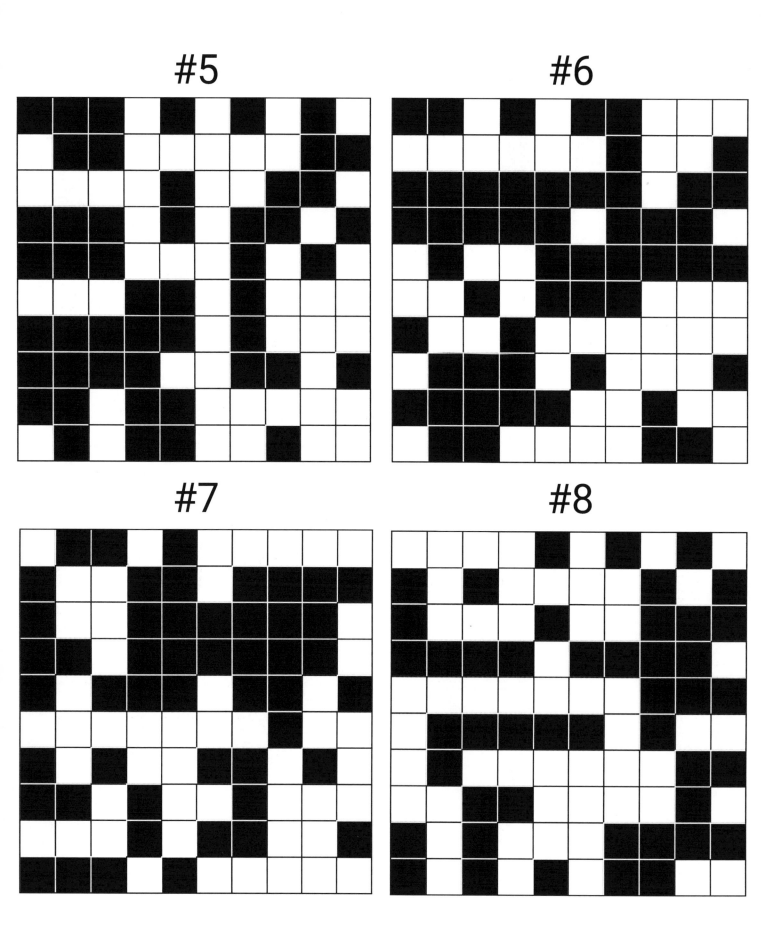

#5

#6

#7

#8

#9

#10

#11

#12

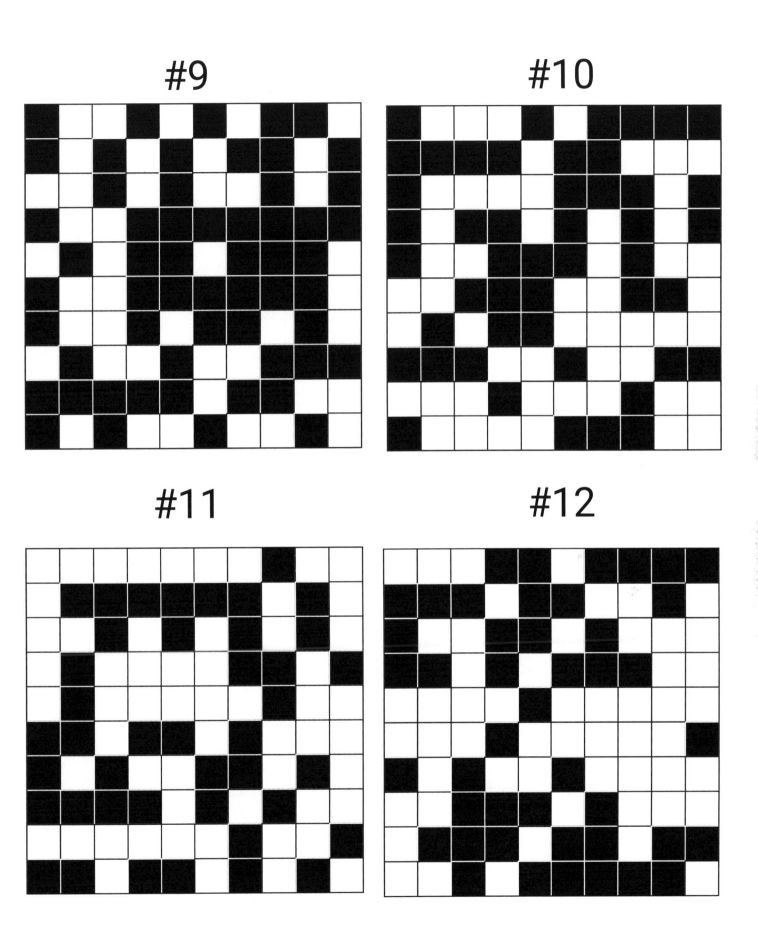

#13

#14

#15

#16

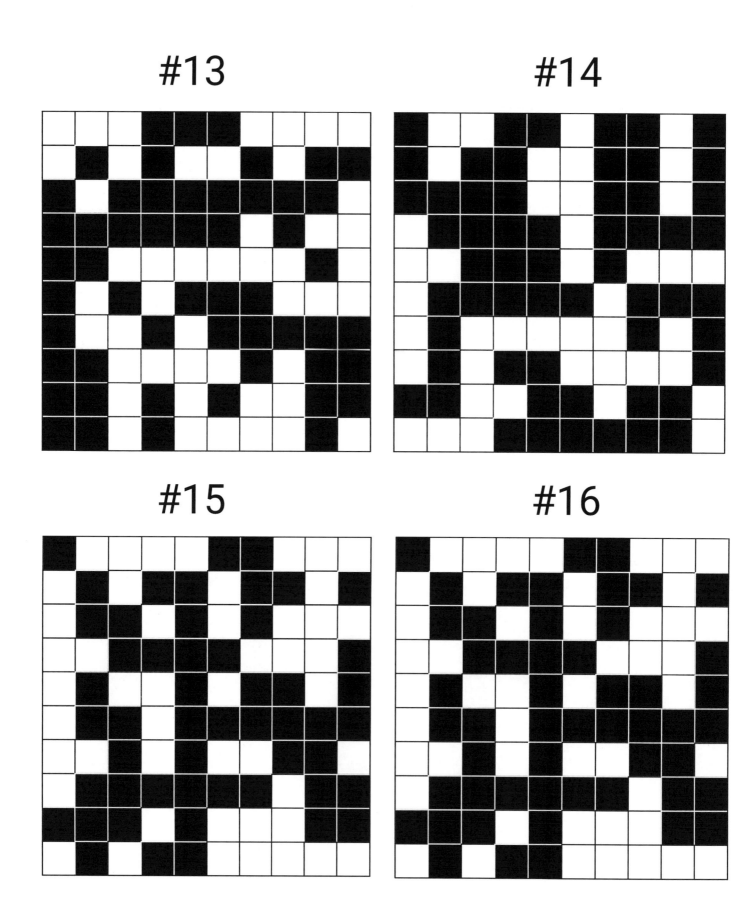

#17

#18

#19

#20

Symbol Math

Each Symbol Math puzzle consists of 5 equations. Each equation comprises 3 symbols, each of which is given a number that, when added to the last number, gives the final number of the equation. Symbols can equate to double-digit numbers.

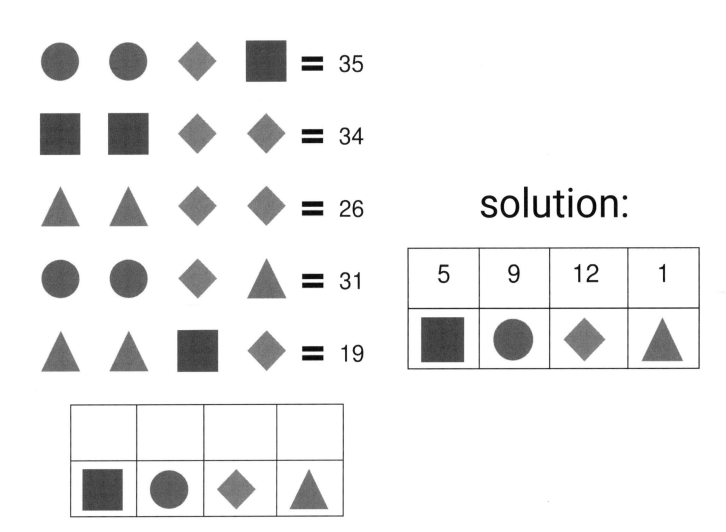

solution:

5	9	12	1
■	●	◆	▲

#1

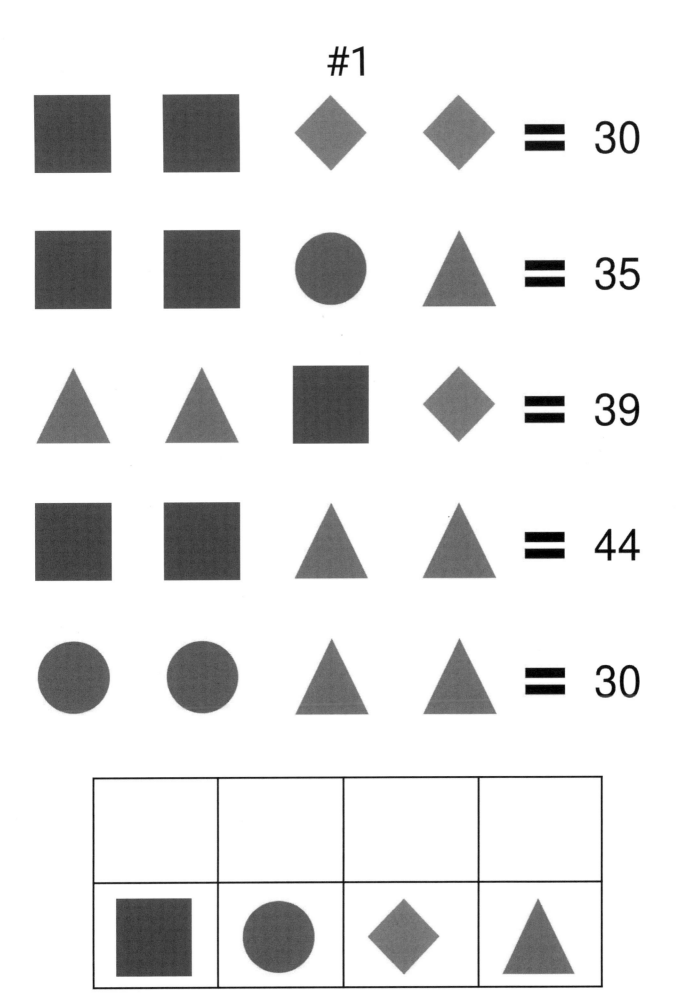

99

#2

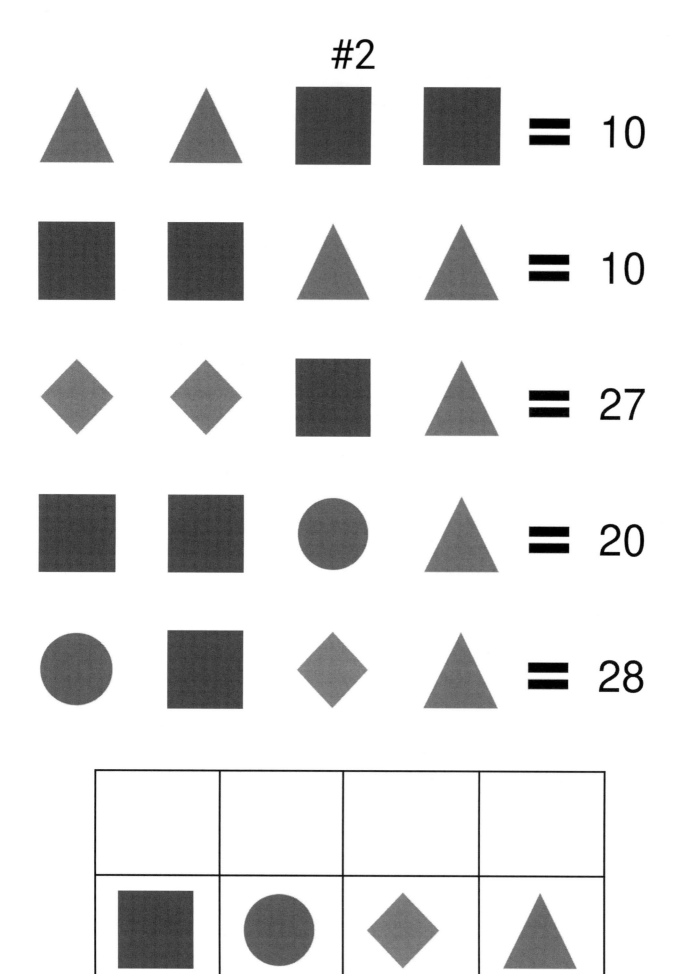

100

#3

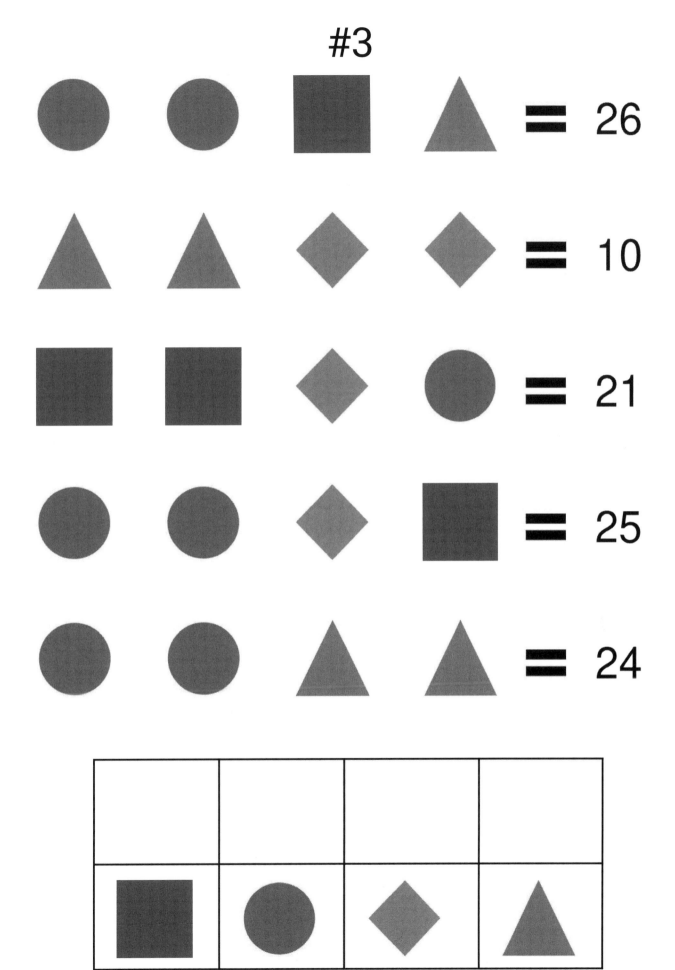

#4

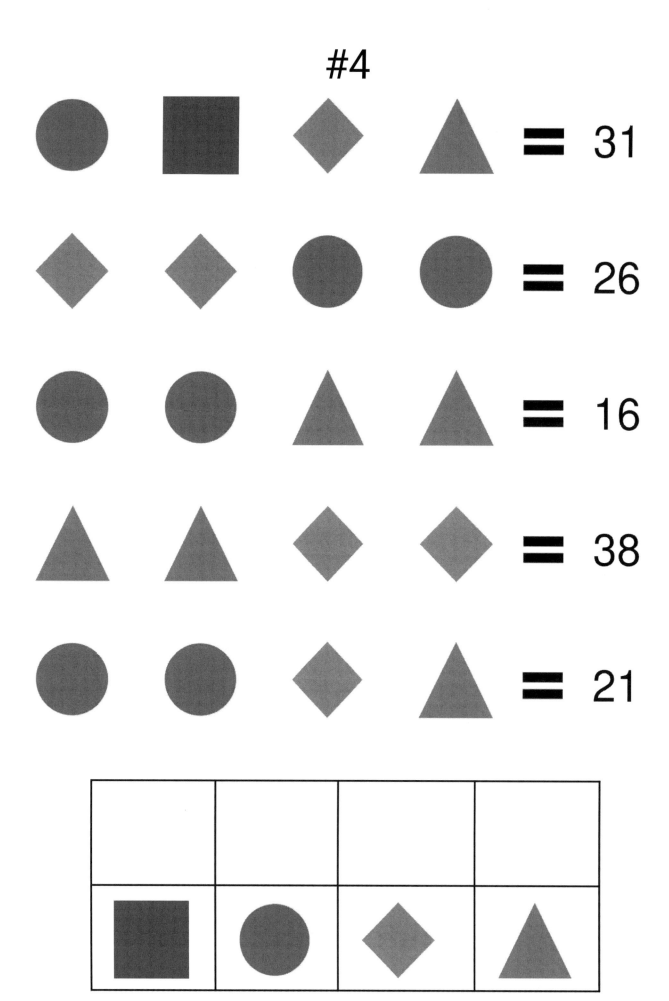

#5

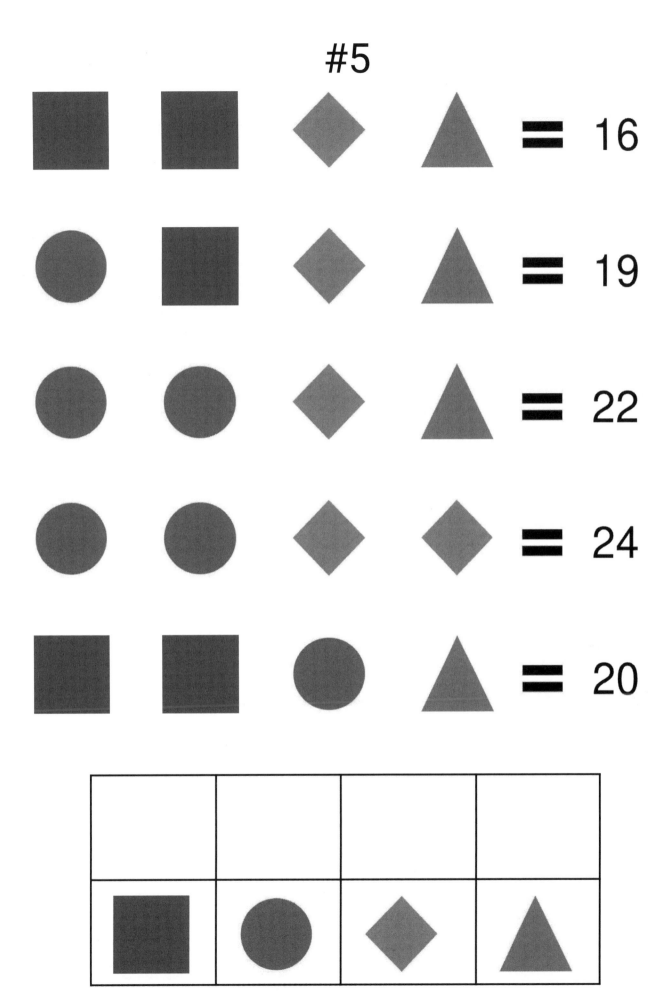

#6

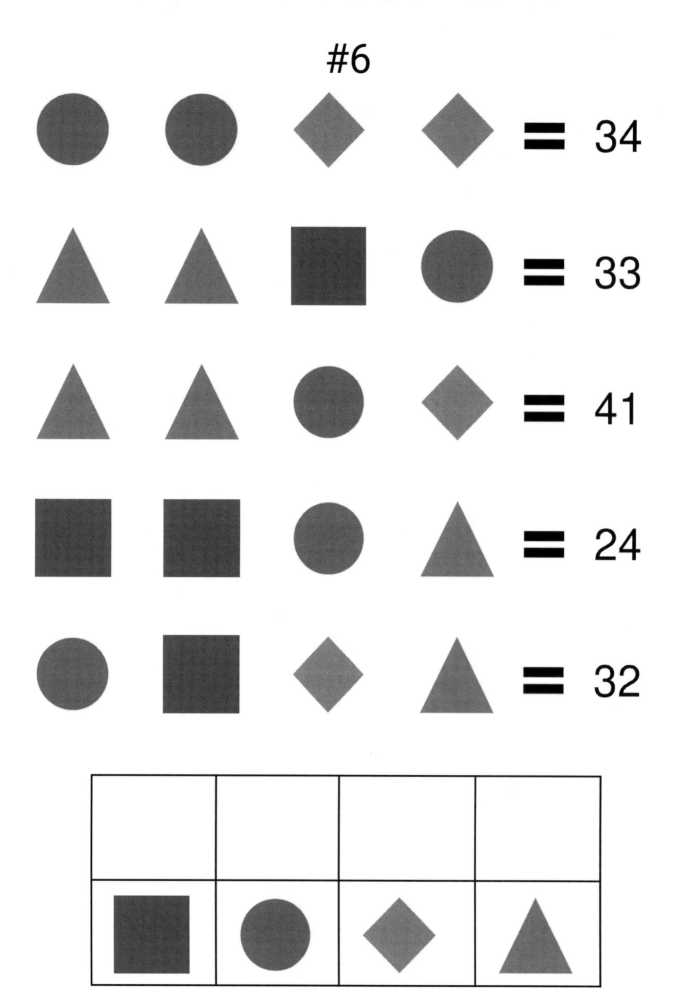

104

#7

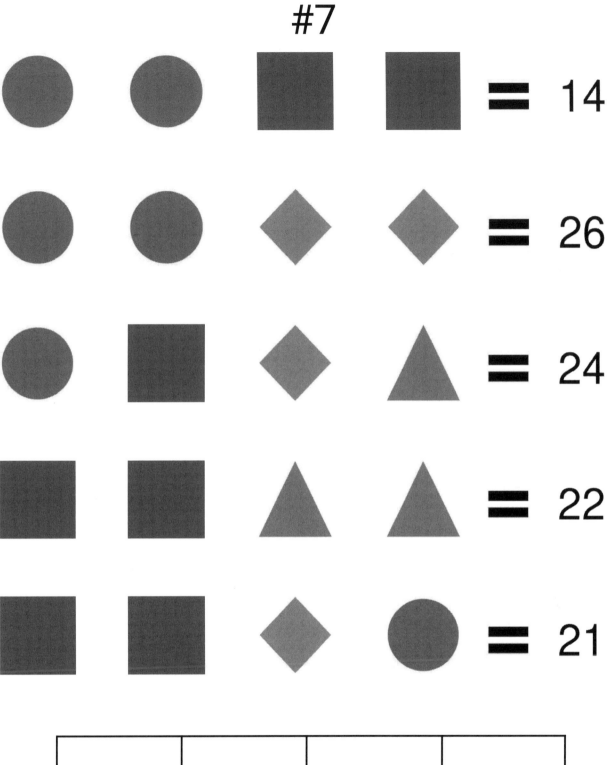

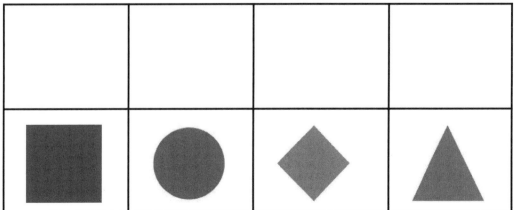

#8

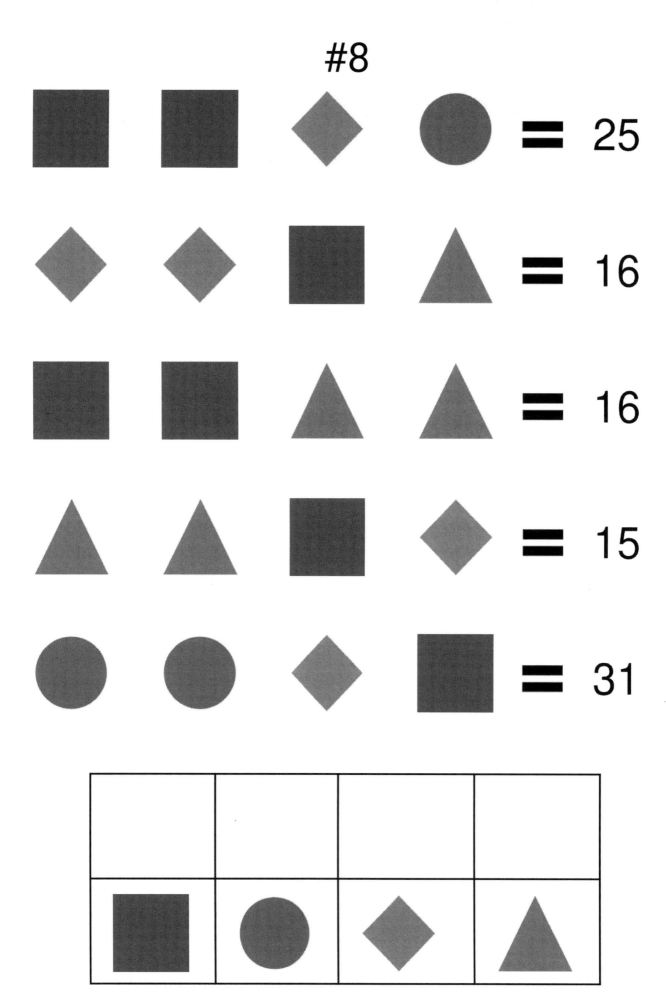

#9

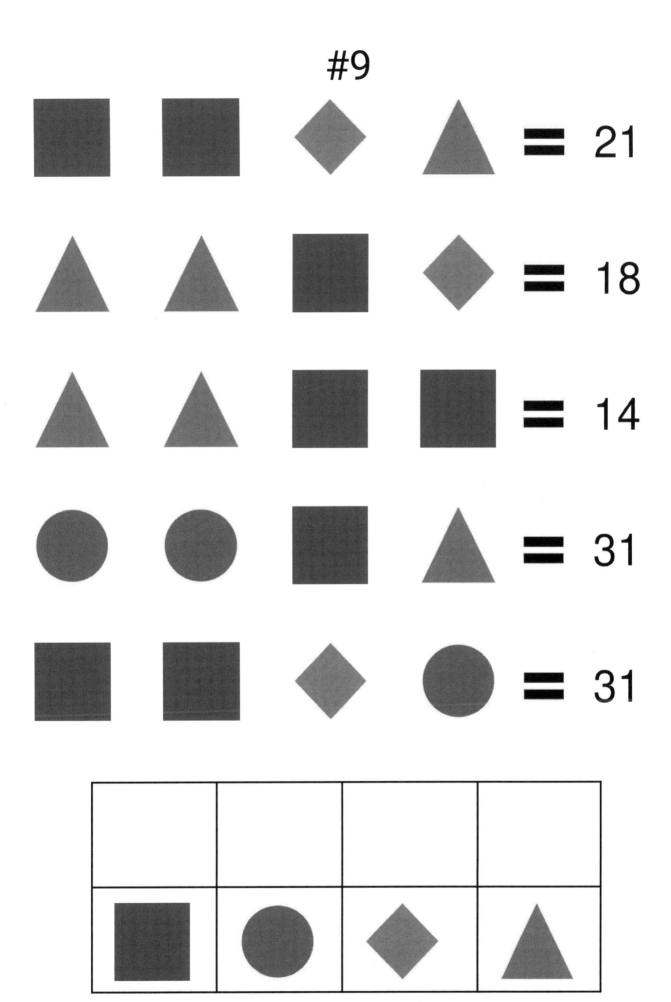

107

#10

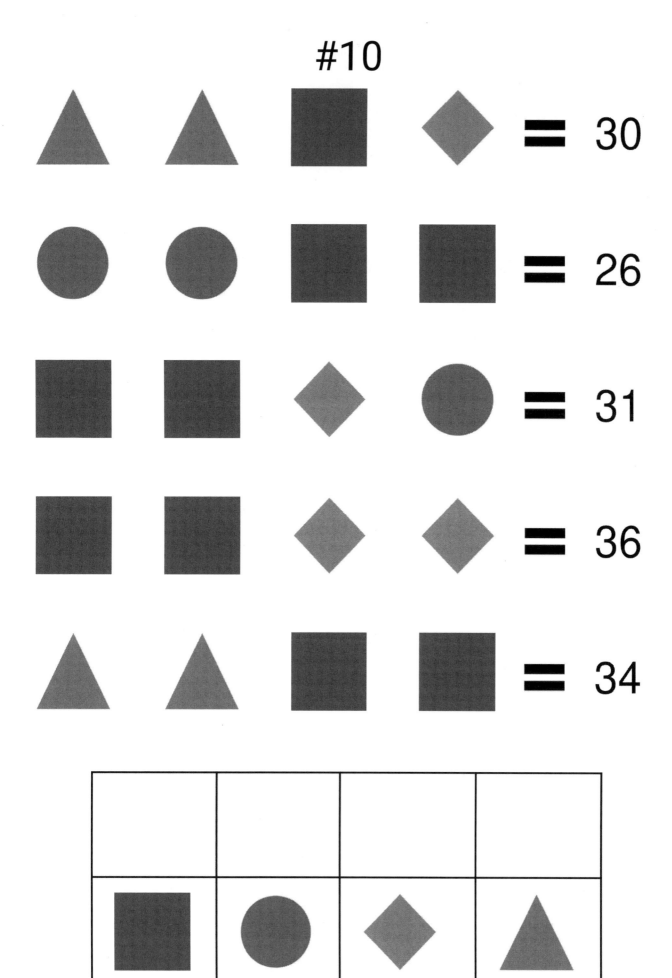

108

#11

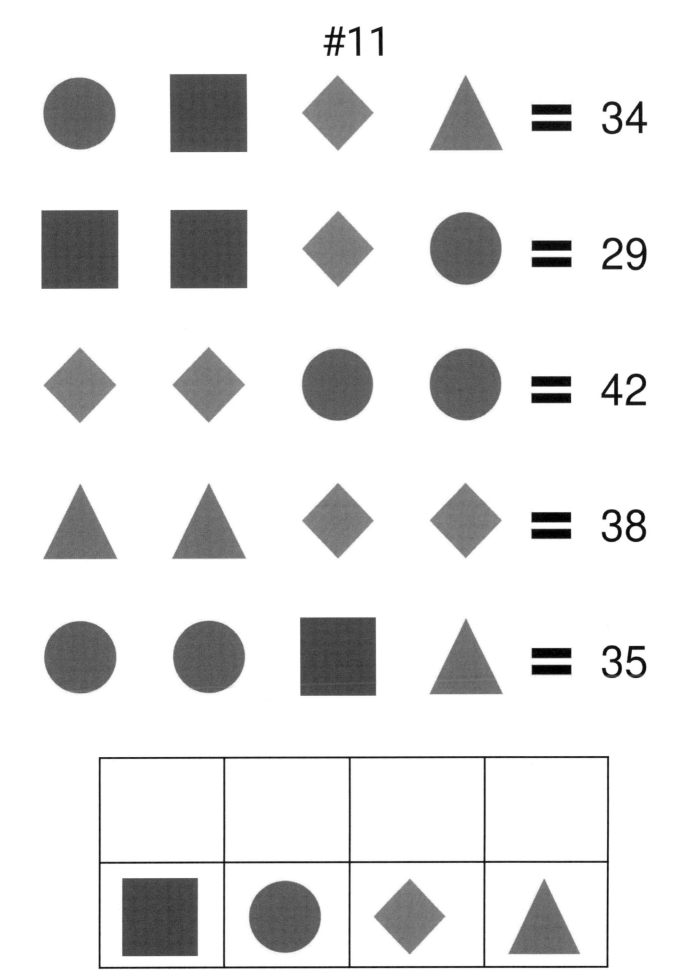

#12

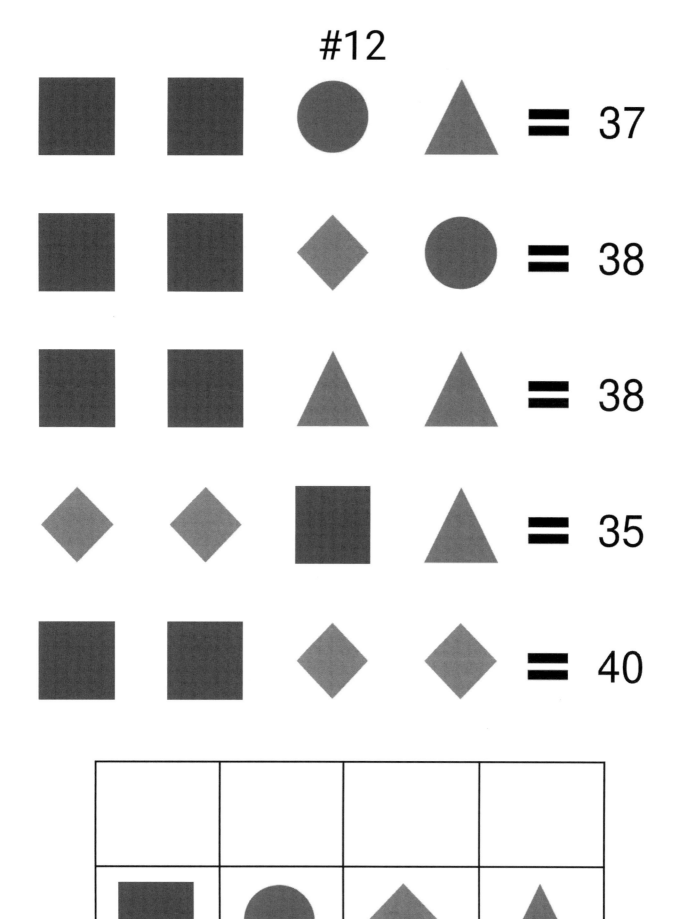

#13

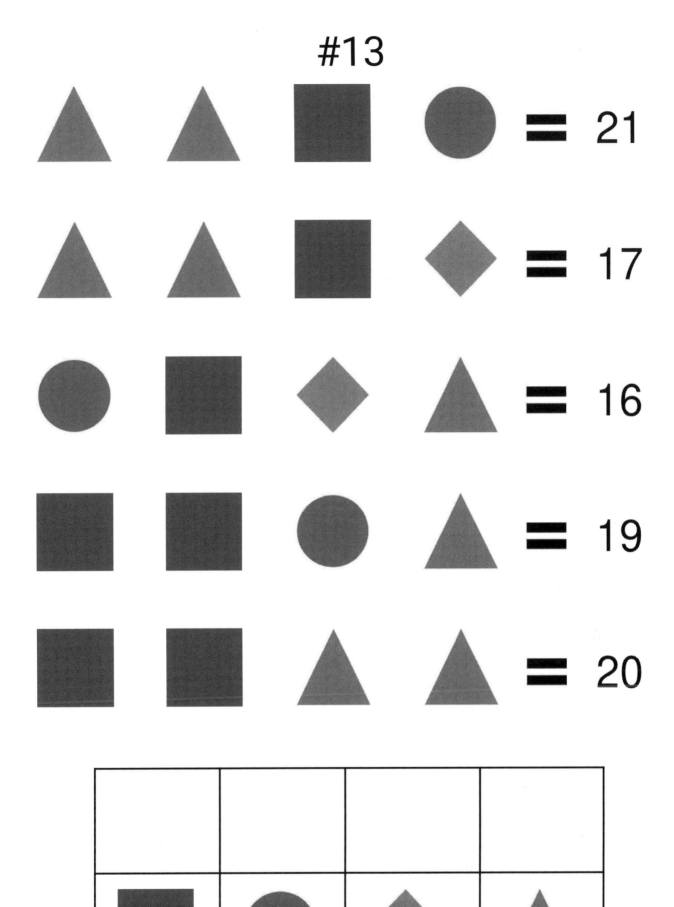

#14

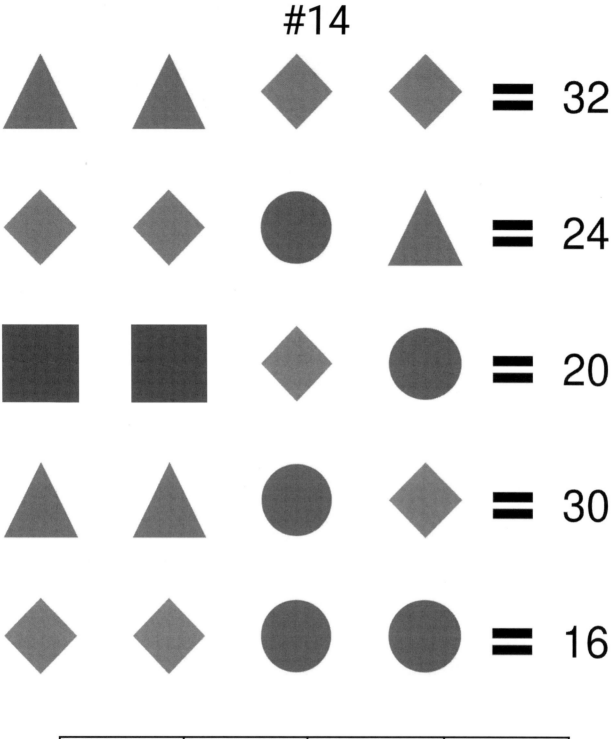

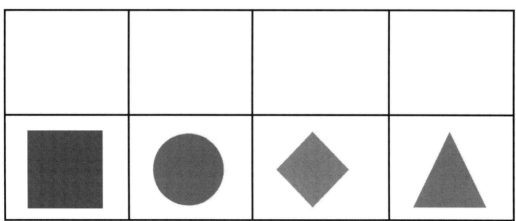

#15

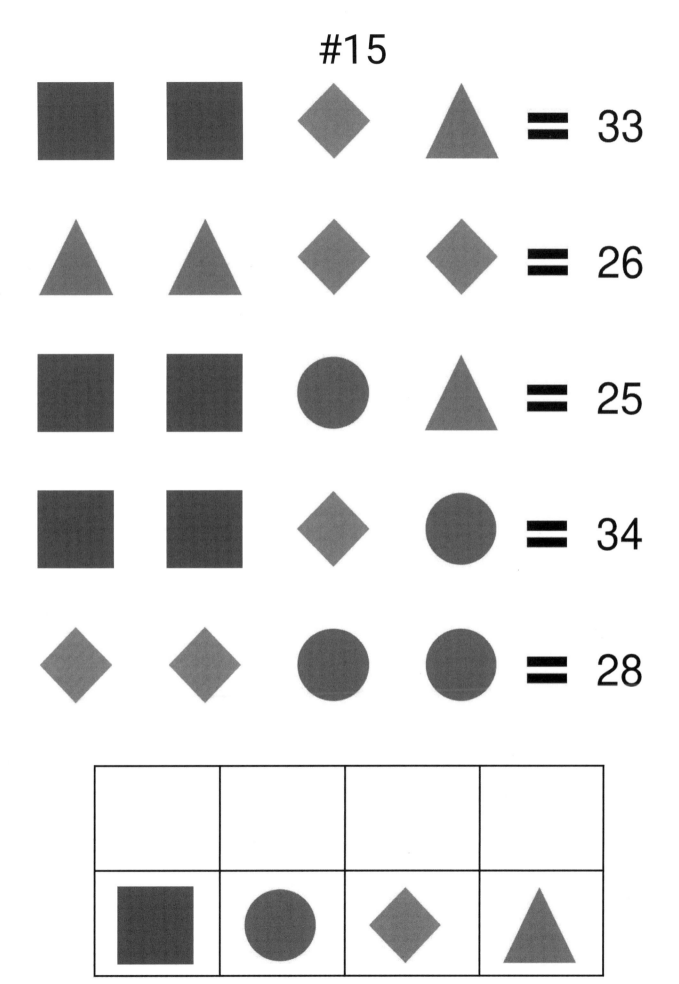

#16

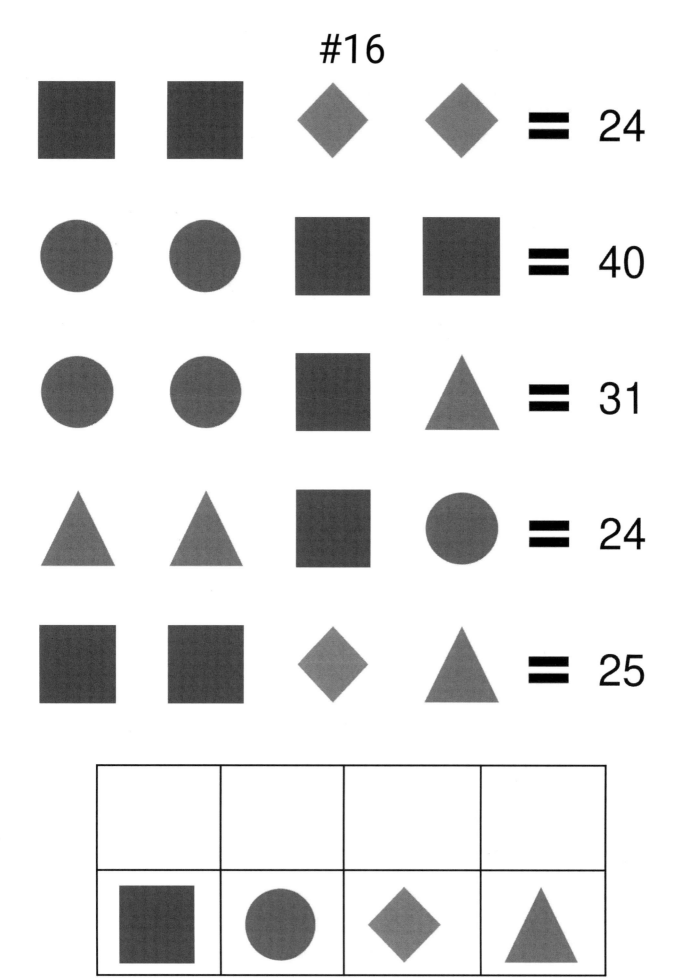

#17

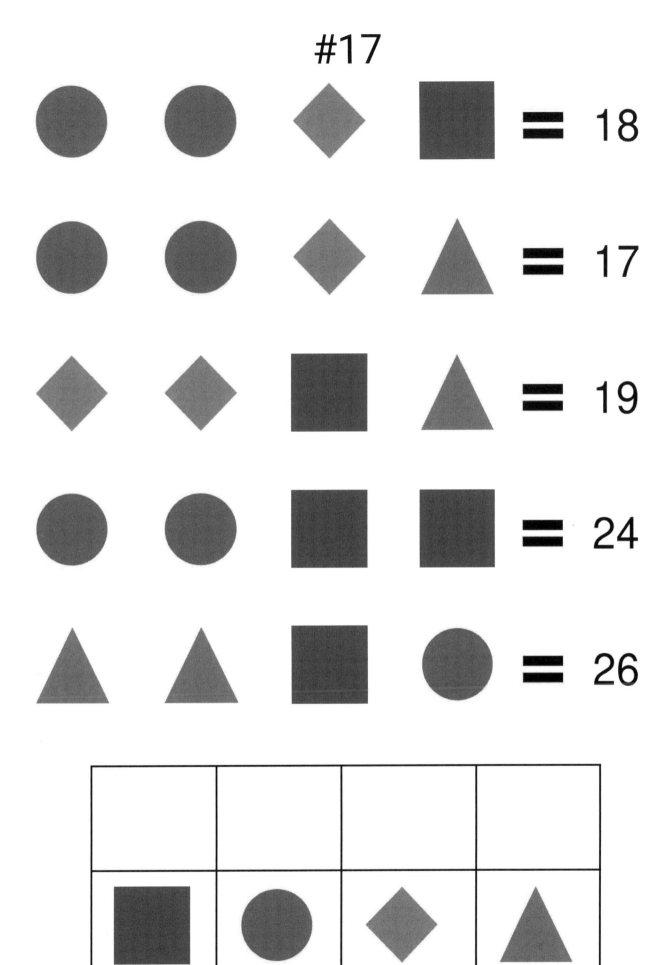

#18

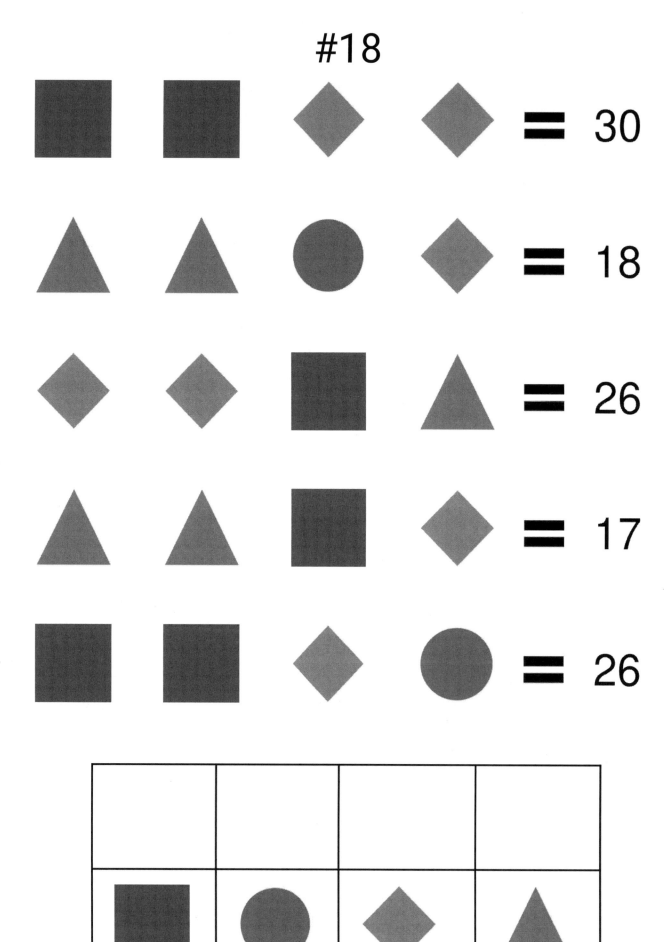

116

#19

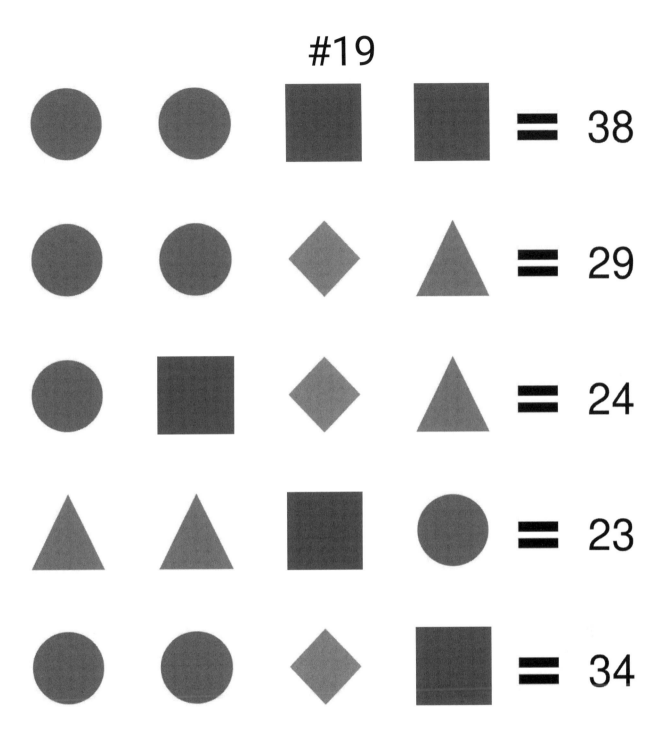

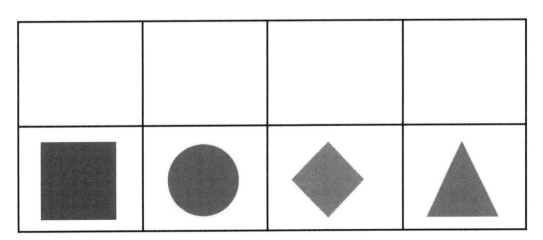

117

#20

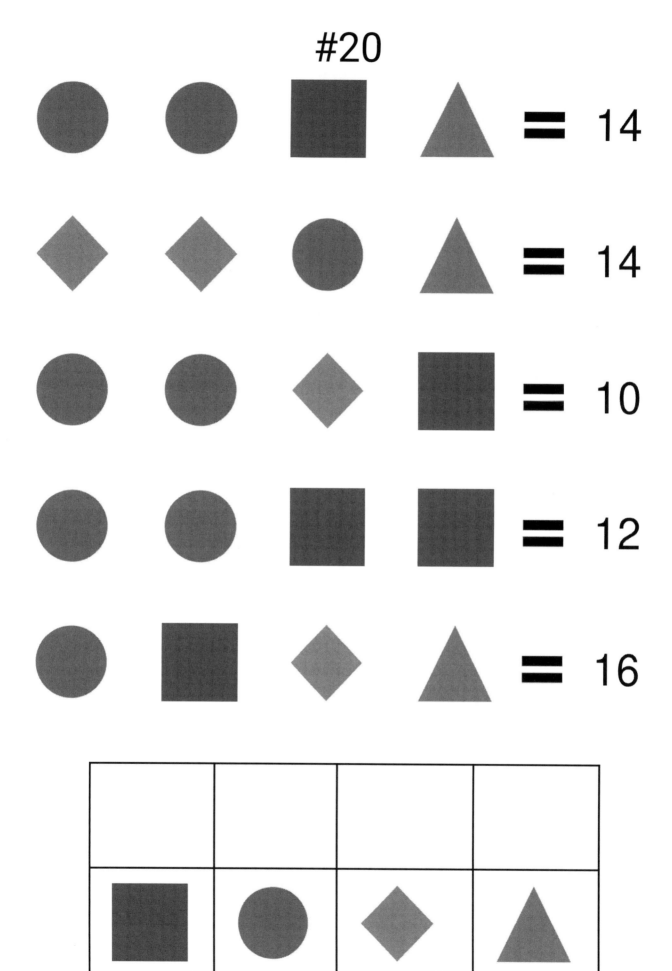

#1

10	3	5	12
■	●	◆	▲

#6

3	6	11	12
■	●	◆	▲

#2

3	12	11	2
■	●	◆	▲

#7

4	3	10	7
■	●	◆	▲

#3

5	9	2	3
■	●	◆	▲

#8

5	11	4	3
■	●	◆	▲

#4

11	1	12	7
■	●	◆	▲

#9

5	12	9	2
■	●	◆	▲

#5

5	8	4	2
■	●	◆	▲

#10

11	2	7	6
■	●	◆	▲

#11

4	11	10	9
■	●	◆	▲

#16

11	9	1	2
■	●	◆	▲

#12

12	6	8	7
■	●	◆	▲

#17

8	4	2	7
■	●	◆	▲

#13

4	5	1	6
■	●	◆	▲

#18

5	6	10	1
■	●	◆	▲

#14

6	3	5	11
■	●	◆	▲

#19

7	12	3	2
■	●	◆	▲

#15

10	3	11	2
■	●	◆	▲

#20

5	1	3	7
■	●	◆	▲

Printed in Great Britain
by Amazon

12839921R00075